Coordination in the Field of Science and Technology – The Role of the Specialized Agencies of UN

Proceedings of the 26th Nobel Symposium
Oslo, September 17–19, 1973

Edited by
August Schou
Director, The Norwegian Nobel Institute

and

Finn Sollie
Director, The Fridtjof Nansen Foundation at Polhøgda

UNIVERSITETSFORLAGET
Oslo 1974

ISBN 82-00-02333-8

SCANDINAVIAN UNIVERSITY BOOKS
Universitetsforlaget, Oslo/Bergen/Tromsø
Munksgaard, Copenhagen
Esselte Studium, Stockholm/Gothenburg/Lund

Printed in Norway by
A.s Joh. Nordahls Trykkeri, Oslo

CONTENTS

OPENING ADDRESS

August Schou, The Norwegian Nobel Institute, Oslo

On behalf of the Norwegian Nobel Institute I have the honour and pleasure to welcome you to this Symposium.

The subject we have chosen may seem almost terrifying in its dimensions. And indeed — we cherish no illusions about the possibilities of an exhaustive analysis during the three days we have at our disposal. What we have in mind is to start a fruitful exchange of ideas and experiences by persons who through many years have been engaged in these problems. We are happy that practically all invited accepted our invitation.

The next exciting phase in the preparations for a symposium is, as you know, the question whether a satisfactory number of participants are willing to deliver speeches as a starting point for the discussions. We appreciate very much that in this respect we fairly soon got positive answers, and that within a short time the abstracts dropped in like the golden rain into the lap of Danae.

The title of our symposium 'Coordination in the Field of Science and Technology' is indeed in good harmony with the spirit of Alfred Nobel. The five prizes he founded were in themselves an expression of his untiring quest for coordination, for synthesis. The activities rewarded by the prizes, he always perceived as a whole: science, literature, and peace work should together make a decisive contribution to the reform of human conditions and at the same time stimulate the sense of tolerance and fraternity. In an extraordinary way Alfred Nobel felt so to say physically the fateful gap in our civilization — the contrast between advanced science and technology on the one hand and on the other hand the low level of general ideas and morality. This fact has often been stressed in the speeches at the Nobel award ceremonies, even before 1914.

Generally speaking I should think that the usual presentation of the old days as an epoch characterized by an unshakeable faith in an automatic progress is not quite true. Even before the first World War many scientists, authors, and philanthropists were aware of the fact that the way towards a better world would be narrow and thorny. Perhaps one might say that just this recognition was among the factors urging them to make their contribution to the benefit of mankind. Some of them undoubtedly — like Nobel himself — represented a fascinating mixture of optimism and pessimism, of sober perseverance and the spirit of deeds and dreams. Among the peace prize winners, I should in this connection like to mention Fridtjof Nansen, whose home we will visit tomorrow.

The world of learning has, as you know, long been characterized by a deplorable split between natural sciences and humanities, — 'the two cultures' in the expression of C. P. Snow. Several outstanding personalities have tried to bridge this gap. In this connection I should like to pay tribute to the memory of our friend Arne Tiselius, the inspiring leader of the cross-cultural Nobel symposium 14 in Stockholm in 1969, who until he died in 1971 worked hard to make the ideas of the symposium a living reality. It is our hope that the discussions here might prove a contribution in the same direction. And with these words I declare the 26th Nobel Symposium to be opened.

THE NEED OF AN INTERNATIONAL POLICY FOR THE SCIENCES

Jean Gottmann, Oxford University

1

It is with a feeling of some awe that I give this first paper at the Nobel Symposium that will discuss the role of the U.N. Specialized Agencies in the international co-ordination of science and technology. I can't help remembering how, in the Spring of 1946, being then Director of Studies and Research in the Department of Social Affairs of the United Nations Secretariat, I spoke about the aims and projects of my small division to a pretty young woman who said she worked for the *New York Times.* Three days later *The New York Times* carried an article entitled 'The United Nations to marshal world science.' Now I want to be more circumspect.

The desire for international agreement and understanding leading to common policies in the field of science and technology for the public good may be ranked as an old aspiration of mankind. In fact, substantial results have been achieved in special areas of particular concern for everyman: for instance, in the circulation of mail, which must have been considered a complex technological matter at the time the Universal Postal Union was established (1874—75), or in epidemiological control, a more obvious concern of science.

Some of us may have had hopes that international policies for the whole range of the sciences would develop after the United Nations discussed the Secretary General's Report on International Laboratories of Scientific Research (1946—49) or when UNESCO and WHO took their first steps (1948—52). We find ourselves still far from any systematic elaboration of co-ordinated policies in this field. Communication between people working in science and technology has been enormously expanded and improved in the last quarter of a century: international research teams, international professional meetings abound. Most of them, however, are sponsored by persons or institutions representing special or national interests. As a result of the sum total of all these activities and of the increasingly interwoven communications between the professions and between the various parts of the world, the positive products of it all emerge and spread on the international scene.

Should we be satisfied with the existing somewhat chaotic dynamics through which contemporary scientific and technological progress is achieved and its products applied to practical purposes? Or should we strive to improve international co-ordination in these matters at a time that seems to be demanding it urgently? The urgency stems from the momentous evolution of this century. The increase in the numbers of the earth's population, which has caused so much worry, is only one of the major factors exerting new pressures on the physical, social, and governmental structures of our planet. While its numbers are rapidly rising, mankind is also re-shaping its habitat through migration, and urbanization; it is re-tooling itself, overhauling its whole equipment; it is also steadily increasing the quantities of material goods consumed *per capita*.

These changes have largely been made possible by the recently acquired capability of science and technology to recast the living and working conditions of mankind. As a geographer I have been concerned for more than a third of a century with the rapid modifications occurring in the environment and in the settlement of the planet. Now these matters have emerged as primary concerns of national governments, and the United Nations after the Stockholm Conference on the Human Environment (1972) is sponsoring a Conference to be held in 1976 in Vancouver on human settlements, a subject even more heavily loaded with vested interests and political dynamite than environmental controls *per se*.

The time seems indeed ripe for a good discussion of the possibility of institutionalizing the elaboration of co-ordinated international policies in the field of science and technology.

2

I should like to stress the changes that at present sharpen the need for an international policy to orient scientific work. These changes fall into two categories: on the one hand, those trends inherent in the evolution of science; on the other hand, those affecting the welfare of mankind and the conduct of international relations.

The first category encompasses such significant trends as the following:

(1) The gradually increasing and improving ability of science and technology to manipulate the physical components of the environment;

(2) The growing capacity of science and technology to influence the behaviour of individuals and of large masses of people;

(3) The constantly self-refining specialization and division of labour within science and technology resulting from the recent expansion and progress achieved in various fields of scientific work;

(4) The greater complementarity between the proliferating specializations, especially when it comes to practical applications, in vivo;

(5) The greater difficulty of communication between and co-ordination of all these specialities, increasingly interdependent in terms of basic thought but increasingly scattered and overwhelmed by their own variety and by the numbers of people, places, responsibilities and problems involved.

By their consequences, the foregoing trends have often impaired in practice, rather than advanced, the use of the products of scientific work and knowledge for the alleviation of the ills and tensions in various parts of the world. The forces of change in the midst of mankind, as they operate in vivo, are compounding the problems and frictions between regions and nations. This seems to be true amid developed nations as much as in the underdeveloped countries.

The second category of trends of change includes such recent developments as the following:

(6) The proliferation of independent national states, causing more autonomy and competition to develop between a larger number of different geographical units, and consequently increasing the number of responsible administrations.

(7) The increase in the demand for consumption of a constantly growing variety of goods and services, due to demographic and economic growth.

(8) The increasing interdependence of the various regional and national units for supply and marketing, as expressed by the expansion of international trade in volume, value, and diversity.

(9) The scope of migratory currents around the world, including internal migrations within countries.

(10) The concentration of populations in urban areas, with thickening high densities on small sections of territory while on vast expanses of inhabitable space densities are thinning out, causing imbalances, tensions, but also regional specialization and more potential complementarity.

(11) The rapid economic progress of certain countries, accentuating the contrast between the lagging parts of the world and the more economically advanced, and preparing more tension, migration and conflicts of interest.

(12) Despite some geographical spread of major facilities of scientific and technological work, the concentration of these facilities and of the related personnel in a small number of areas.

(13) The lack of understanding by the more privileged sections of the actual needs and potential resources of the poorer sectors.

More direct contacts to discuss and try to shape common scientific policies could be institutionalized.

(14) Automation and rationalization in all branches of production work and of some tertiary activities, changing employment prospects and making it imperative to re-orient the large masses of people who are entering or will soon join the labour force in various countries.

(15) The rapidly expanding role of maritime space for a variety of uses.

(16) The growing use of the space above the planet's surface for a variety of activities that can hardly be confined to one nation's territorial space.

(17) The extraordinary improvement in the distribution of information, with its disregard of distances and political boundaries.

(18) The growing belief that environmental and social circumstances can be modified by concerted human action — and the consequent desire for greater equality among large masses of people.

3

The trends of change enumerated above are all inter-related as factors affecting the fields of science, economics, and politics; they concur in pointing out the need to organize on the international level. Such organization could take on various forms and could well use the channels of existing institutions, especially of the Specialized Agencies of the United Nations. However, any co-ordination between these institutions and between the more far-flung networks of national authorities and professional groups and institutes could hardly be seriously undertaken unless it is meant to carry out an agreed-upon policy.

Past experience seems to indicate that international policy may be agreed upon as guidelines for action needed to resolve an urgent situation that threatens the well-being, physical or economic, of large numbers of people in several nations. The best progress has been achieved, I believe, in the field of public health: when an epidemic threatens, international agreement for concerted action is usually secured without much difficulty in order to arrest the spread of the disease. Similarly, it may be argued that the Postal Union removed the threat of possible isolation.

Governments are moved to act and even to compromise national differences in order to provide for the well-being of their people. And this well-being in a time of world expansion requires provision of security and of some opportunity. On the morrow of the Second World War an international consensus was reached on a few general principles concerning the need for a redistribution of the economic means of production, including qualified technical personnel, between the richer and the poorer countries. To some extent this policy was applied and the aid to the developing countries certainly improved an evolution of the world which would have been much more difficult and more unpleasant without it.

The precedents in the fields of public health and of economic policy may be indicative of what could be attempted for science and technology. For instance, there have been recurrent threats of shortages in various categories of goods, either food or energy or some kinds of minerals; lately, a serious shortage seems to be looming in as ordinary a raw material as the aggregates needed for the manufacture of concrete, and this shortage threatens, especially in Europe, a basic supply of the construction industry and, indirectly, the provision of housing. All such shortages contribute to the rise of prices and therefore to inflation, besides the more direct hardships that may be caused.

There is little doubt that science and technology could alleviate much of these difficulties if, with due notice given for the research to be done and about its results, general attention were given not only to means of increasing the production of goods in short supply, but also to means of economizing the quantities of materials used to obtain the goods neeeded to satisfy the consumers' demand. Our Western civilization has encouraged on the whole the waste of material resources in the process of 'economic progress'. Much pollution and speculation could be avoided if an international consensus oriented scientific research towards methods and processes saving quantities of raw materials. Past experience shows, in several branches of production, from power houses to television sets and even automobiles, that consumption may be adequately provided for, while quantities of materials used to supply each consumer are reduced either by miniaturization or by more economic methods of raw material (or fuel) use.

Additional savings may be achieved by a greater endeavour to find use for by-products in manufacturing processes. I have long marvelled at the admirable results obtained by Swiss and Swedish industries in transforming the waste of breweries, that used to pollute the rivers, into high protein feed for poultry, cattle, and even — at a slightly higher cost — for humans. I have also wondered at the very small number of places that have taken advantage of that technique. But many more useful 'gadgetries' of this kind could be obtained if a decisive impulse was given by international policy to science in favour of research oriented to saving materials.

It may be possible to draw guidelines for the use of existing scientific knowledge in the pursuit of internationally desirable and accepted goals. I have mentioned a few in areas with which I am somewhat familiar; many other suggestions could certainly be offered by other specialists. The present fluidity of the distribution of people, their resources and activities on the globe has acquired a dynamism never before attained. It was not really expected; it has been only partly surveyed and recorded. Many of our present tensions, conflicts, and discomforts stem from the suddenness of this fluidity. It opens new opportunities and also it threatens chaos; we could avoid the latter and exploit the former by concerted action once a few general principles for such action are ironed out.

The possibility of freeing themselves from the shackles of traditional structures — geographical, economic, and social — was brought to people mostly by the recent innovations of science and technology, and also by rapid political and ethical evolution. Politics and ethics could perhaps have reacted somewhat differently than they did to the opportunity afforded by the advances of science. But science could also orient its concerns along different tracks of thought. Amid the pressures resulting from the prevailing fluidity some indication of choices could steer scientists towards work on the more urgent needs of mankind. This occurs in the usual course of events every time a serious crisis shatters a nation or a group of nations; even when such a crisis is resolved in a part of the world, it usually leaves scars on some aspect of international relations.

Could this historical process be improved by adoption of an international policy for science? In any case, the extreme dynamism of the present fluidity threatens to bring about rather chaotic endeavours in many directions, with much duplication and misunderstanding. At least some loss of highly qualified work and some unpleasantness could be avoided if an international agreement on general guidelines, including priorities and options, were to be offered. International agreements have a tradition of outlining mainly regulations and rules of a restrictive nature. A policy for science could perhaps agree on what could be done rather than on what should not be tried. A more positive than restrictive approach could be more acceptable to scientific personnel.

The growing dependence of a higher proportion of mankind on science and technology for daily critical requirements is sometimes associated with the metaphor of a 'shrinking world'. It seems, in fact, that scientific and technological work proceeds in an expanding world: each of us, as an individual, has to deal with a constantly growing number of people, in more places, to gather the data, information, and advice we need; every country deals with a growing number of places, people, institutions, and concepts. This expansion of our private and public universe requires more ordering, classification, guidelines. Scientists would certainly resist any attempt to marshal world science; they might welcome the establishment of a recognized marshalling yard for needs and resources.

Last but not least, the time seems ripe for an international policy because the apparent order which existed after 1945, owing to the high concentration of science and technology in a very small number of countries and centres, has now been eroded. If any international policy for science has been operating in the last 20 years, it has certainly been one of geographic decentralization. It has borne results; one consequence of it is precisely the need for more common moorings.

PROBLEMS OF COORDINATION

Finn Sollie, The Fridtjof Nansen Foundation at Polhøgda, Norway

The purpose of this paper is to focus attention on major problems and difficulties in the international and interdisciplinary coordination in the field of science and technology.

A first and obvious difficulty is that we lack a tradition of international coordination and cooperation in science and technology. Much of the experience that we have got comes from various limited and short-term or stop-gap operations or it is related to a war effort and arms technology. One problem is that so much of the international effort that we have had so far for coordinated research and development has been directed at *preventing* things, rather than at *creating* new solutions and developments. Programs under the World Health Organization, for example, have been successful in fighting and preventing disease, but they have hardly provided the kind of experience and expertise that is required for international programs to create new solutions, e.g. by removing such old causes of disease as hunger and malnutrition and such modern causes of death and suffering as traffic accidents and pollution. Experience from large-scale programs in arms technology for obvious reasons may be quite irrelevant to problems that are of a civilian nature and concern the every-day life and well-being of men and nations and where the goal is to be productive rather than destructive.

A second difficulty is that the problem of coordination in science and technology is so closely tied in with fundamental political and economic problems and issues. In this Nobel Symposium we may indulge in the luxury of rational discussion and dispassionate analysis of needs for and advantages of coordination in research and development. However, the needs which can and must be met through a better coordinated scientific effort and international cooperation in technological development must also be understood in their political and economic context. It is important to note this, because it means that no large-scale scheme or effort of international coordination in science and technology can work effectively unless there are legitimate political motives, as well as strong scientific and technical reasons for the effort. An effective program must have a political, as well as a scientific logic. One problem in this connection is that all

14

too often the world of science and the world of politics appear to be poles apart and that in analyzing identical problems from their opposite positions, scientists and politicians reach opposite conclusions. Often, there will be strong political reasons for avoiding or even preventing programs for which there are very strong scientific reasons. Some examples will illustrate how difficult it may be to get the necessary political support for programs that we know are needed from a scientific point of view.

In the case of our natural environment, we know that there is an urgent need to develop new industrial techniques and processes that are less destructive of the environment than are many of the processes currently in use throughout the world. There is hardly a need to emphasize this point, which scientists can prove with impeccable logic and frightening detail. Most states, and certainly most industrial states, agree that it is important and necessary to do research for improved technology in order to save the environment. These states see a need for setting up international programs and defining rigid international standards. Some states, however, especially among the underdeveloped countries which have not yet had the advantages or the disadvantages of industrialization, will object to participating in any such international effort to introduce new processes and standards. One basic reason for their objection in this respect is that the new technologies which are needed to meet the requirements and standards of advanced industrial states will be more costly and thus make it even more difficult for the underdeveloped countries to improve their own economy. In their case, therefore, pollution and other environment dangers will seem to present a smaller risk than continued underdevelopment. There is a good deal of sound political logic in the argument that countries which are only now entering the age of industrialization should not be called upon to introduce more sophisticated and expensive equipment and processes in order that they may help to alleviate the problems that have been created by nations which have become rich through a technology which they now want to prohibit. In this situation, a globally coordinated effort and a universal standard hardly appear to be a working possibility, at least unless a parallel scheme is adopted to compensate developing countries for the added cost. Needless to say, such a scheme will involve difficulties of its own that may further complicate the task of creating an international environment program for industry.

In a similar manner, different industrial states may have opposite priorities and objectives in their development policy. Thus, today a number of states make wide use of nuclear energy and produce vast and increasing amounts of radioactive waste. Some of these states are now looking toward Antarctica as a possible site for storing this waste. Other nations have opposite objectives and want to maintain Antarctica as a nature reserve e.g. by upholding the present ban in the Antarctic Treaty against the disposing of radioactive material in the frozen continent. How can one coordinate the development of technology in a nation looking forward to getting rid of its waste in Antarctica with the development in a nation looking forward to protecting Antarctica forever against any such use?

The different political and economic priorities of underdeveloped and industrialized countries will also affect policy on the management of resources. While many of the industrialized nations see a need to prevent waste and to make more effective use of limited resources, for instance by recycling and developing substitutes for scarce resources, other nations, especially in the underdeveloped part of the world, which are producers of raw materials will be opposed to the development of a technology that may reduce the demand for their own products. Often their short-term needs will cause such opposition even if they are clearly aware of the fact that their own resources and hence their source of income are limited.

There is one area today where the world has a magnificent opportunity for scientific coordination and technological cooperation. This is ocean space, which is the hugest natural reserve that has not yet been exploited and despoiled by man. In the Law of the Sea Conference we also have the advantage of a legal and political forum for developing an international system for the exploration and exploitation of ocean space. Setting up such a system, however, which will be a new creation in international law and politics, is a difficult task, and the nations which are involved, that is the full membership of the United Nations, often have disparate and opposite interests. The very difficulty of setting up a new system for ocean space may cause us to lose this opportunity to create for the first time a truly coordinated international effort on a large scale in the field of science and technology. Even if it should prove possible to harmonize the interests of the various states the task of reaching an agreement may take so long that the result will in the end be totally ineffective. The reason for this is that experiments are already being conducted to extract minerals from the deep sea bed. If these experiments are successful we may expect a veritable gold-rush on the sea bed. Such a run on the sea bed with competiton between corporations and between states to gain maximum benefits may effectively put an end to all efforts to set up an international regime.

In this situation, an immediate ban or moratorium against exploitation of the deep sea bed is probably the only means by which one can secure sufficient time for reaching a permanent agreement on the management of ocean space. It will not be easy, however, to get a decision for a temporary ban or moratorium. Even in Antarctica, where no more than twelve states are involved in consultation and where profitable exploitation is definitely further off into the future, it is extremely difficult to get an agreement on a moratorium against economic exploitation, in spite of the fact that in Antarctica there is a long tradition of quite close scientific cooperation. In this case, as so often, the political logic which participating states are bound to follow has different conclusions from the scientific logic, which would say that only by adopting a temporary moratorium can one insure that an irreversible development is not begun that in a few years time all will agree should have been stopped.

Obviously, the political difficulties will be determined by the nature and intensity of the national interests which are involved in or affected by any scheme for international coordination in science and technology. It is equally obvious that these difficulties will depend on the scope and objectives of the coordinated program. A distinction can be made here between what we may term *passive* coordination and *active* coordination.

Passive coordination involves limited functions of a relatively technical nature, such as registration, systematization and exchange of information about current programs and research. Its basic characteristic is that initiative for planning, adoption, and execution of programs will not be taken by the coordinating agency, but will remain a responsibility of the scientists themselves, of research institutions and industry, and of national authorities.

In active coordination, on the other hand, a coordinating agency will have some responsibility for reviewing and assessing trends in research and development, for planning, recommending, and conducting programs, and for follow-up. If highly developed, with a number of large-scale programs and established priorities in research and development, coordination will also be an important element in an international science policy. An international science policy, however, will affect important economic and other national interests.

In cases of passive coordination, which is mostly of a technical nature, political issues will not usually arise. On the other hand, when the research and development for which coordination is sought is active in the sense that it is goal-oriented, and especially when economic and other vital national interests are involved, there is indeed a danger that political issues will cause grave difficulties. As an example of this, we may again look at the Antarctic experience, which has gone through distinct phases of development.

17

The first phase in the Antarctic development was marked by the slow and gradual build-up of political tensions as an increasing number of states laid claim to and annexed Antarctic territories. At the time of the Second World War there was tension both between states holding competing claims and between claimant states and states that had not made claims for Antarctic territory and that in principle regarded Antarctica as an international area. After the war attempts were made to find a political solution but these efforts were unsuccessful and, because both the United States and the Soviet Union were involved, there was a danger that the sovereignty dispute might bring Antarctica into the cold war. Then, in connection with the International Geophysical Year (1957—58), scientists from twelve countries, claimant states as well as non-claimant states, moved into Antarctica in a coordinated program of scientific exploration that stands as a model of international cooperation. The basis for this program was a gentleman's agreement reached by the scientists to the effect that their activities in Antarctica should not in any way affect or alter the legal and political situation in the continent. This agreement and the program of scientific cooperation together were so effective that they provided the basis for the Antarctic Treaty (1959), which reaffirmed that scientific cooperation should continue and have no legal or political effects. This second phase which has been marked by close and open cooperation with no legal or political complication may now be drawing to an end because the very scientific exploration which twenty years ago served to defuse the political issues is now producing results that are beginning to attract economic interests. Today, continued scientific exploration is beginning to center on the goal of future economic exploitation of the resources that may be found in Antarctica. As a result we can already see that the governments involved are beginning to think in terms of their potential economic interests and advantages, thus beginning a third phase in the Antarctic development. In this new phase the very system of scientific cooperation which first served to pacify Antarctica and then produced results that promised an economic future for Antarctica may move toward its own break-down if the political issues are not solved. At this stage therefore, a political solution is becoming a pre-condition for continued scientific coordination.

What we have seen in Antarctica is that the scientists themselves were able to act effectively for an improved and coordinated international program. However, we have also seen that when this program begins to produce applicable results and to reach what may properly be called the *technological stage,* new difficulties arise.

From the Antarctic and other experiences we know that political logic, while willing to let scientific reason have its reign when basic research and passive coordination are involved, will want to reassert itself when research becomes applied and economic interests become involved. When this happens we must ask if the scientists will be able to continue their course of close cooperation in spite of adverse political odds. It is perhaps possible that they can do so in Antarctica because there there is a solid tradition for coordinated scientific work. In other instances, however, where no such tradition exists, the advent of the technological stage in research and development will raise some disquieting questions about the ability of scientists to participate in coordinated programs and to cooperate internationally.

I shall not discuss here the personal preferences of the scientists themselves beyond saying that today most scientists are strongly specialized and sectorized in their work and that they, like anyone else, will have personal and institutional preferences for their work. To the extent that a scientist is a free agent, he, like any person with the opportunity to choose, will be antagonistic toward being directed and dictated to. His propensity toward coordination will probably be no stronger than the advantages he can see from participation. In most instances, however, personal preferences are not very important. The majority of our scientists are not free agents, but employees whose services are bought and paid for. Their work is planned and conducted in the service of an employer. The question of coordination, therefore, is not so much one about the wilingness of the scientist himself to be coordinated as it is a question about the willingness of his employer to let his employees work as part of coordinated programs in which several institutions and several nations participate.

In most instances the employers of scientists are government agencies or private industrial concerns. I have already discussed at some length how and why the political logic by which governments act may make international coordination difficult. The next question then is about the role of industry and the need to secure participation and cooperation from industry in the coordinating effort. Because today industry is such a strong and growing international power factor, and because this power is to such a large extent based upon mastery of technology, industry exerts a strong influence upon development and activities in the field of science and technology. This influence may also affect efforts for coordination through UN agencies and other international bodies.

In general terms, we may point to three characteristic features of modern industry which will be a source of tension between the goals and objectives of industry and the goals and purpoes of international coordination in the field of science and technology:

First of all, research and development within the industrial complex is intimately related to specific economic interests. The primary goal is to produce and market products at a profit and this obviously may conflict with the goals and motives for international coordination, which are defined on the basis of wider interests than those of industry or business profit.

Secondly, industry is marked by a high degree of competiton between firms and branches. Research and development provide the best weapons for competition with other firms with similar products, as well as for competition with those who market completely different products that can distract consumer interest. Industrial research and development has a built-in element of secrecy bred by competition that runs contrary to the requirements for the open exchange of information and cooperation that must be followed in any coordinated program.

Thirdly, and in large measure as a result of modern technology, today we have international industrial and economic interdependence to such an extent that we may talk about an international industrial-economic system. This international industrial-economic system functions on its own terms and is not organized as part of the traditional system of states. National governments, which have power and means of control only within their own territory, cannot individually check and control practices and operations within the industrial-economic system that extend beyond national borders, and no parallel international political system has been established that has international controlling powers and functions. It is still difficult to assess the full implications of the development of an increasingly tightly woven international industrial-economic system over which no effective political control is as yet exerted, but it is fair to assume that in any future large-scale effort at international coordination in science and technology, the special interests represented by industry may conflict with the interests which scientists represent and with the interests which politicians represent. Any international program which will adversely affect industrial interests will cause problems unless some liaison and a new degree of cooperation is also established between industry and politics.

In conclusion, we may say that coordination in the field of science and technology, which is in one sense a problem of efficient and effective organization, is in many respects a political problem. Neither problem, that of organization or that of political agreement, has an easy solution, and this may call for a step-by-step approach to the task of improved coordination in science and better cooperation in technological development. No complete system of full-scale international coordination can be envisaged today. However, by concentrating on a few projects, it may be possible to achieve effective coordination in some sectors and to gain experience for broader cooperation in the future.

SOME PRINCIPLES OF AN EFFICIENT DIVISION OF LABOUR IN RESEARCH

Jan Tinbergen, Erasmus University of Rotterdam

1. *Introductory*

The increasing need for scientific research has raised the number of research workers and the amounts spent on research to unprecedented levels. In the developed countries between 1 and 3 per cent of GNP is now spent on research and development; for the USA alone this is of the order of magnitude of 30 billion (in the American sense) dollars. The activities covered are scattered, however, over an enormous number of institutions of widely diverging nature and there is a widefelt need for a better coordination and division of labour as well as for clearer priorities. The fulfilment of this need requires a much higher degree of cooperation, formal or informal, and of planning. There are limits, however, to these means, because among the factors making for success of research, some degree of free choice for the individual scientist is important too. While some rigidity in organization may be called for, a fair degree of mobility of the individual participants should be allowed for and even be stimulated, for instance by uniformity of labour conditions in a number of scientific research institutes.

Some guidelines for an efficient division of labour among scientific institutions around the world can be derived from the logical structure of the tools of research, often organized as 'models'. These guidelines are the subject of this paper.

2. *Multivariate interdisciplinary models needed*

Many sciences have worked with models, some of them for a long time already, for instance physics (models of gases, of light, of sound, of atoms, etc.). A model may be said to be a simplified picture of the aspect of reality studied; simplified, in order to enable the human mind to use it, but maintaining what are assumed to be the 'relevant' elements or features of reality. What is relevant depends on the phase of research and the aims pursued.

Since the future of mankind is at stake, as a consequence of (i) the dangerous nature of armament in existence, (ii) extreme poverty in large parts of the world, (iii) the possible consequences of population growth, (iv) pollution, (v) the exhaustion of energy, and (vi) of other mineral resources, there is a particular need for socio-economic policies able to prevent major disasters like nuclear war, famine, and intoxication, not to speak of the many secondary disasters such as diseases, 'minor' wars, or overcrowding, from happening.

For the solution of problems of socio-economic policies — up to changes in social order and the international order — socio-economic planning models are a possible starting point. Among their advantages are a forty-year experience with them[1] and their degree of adaptability to needs of integrating other scientific realms. In other words, parts of socio-economic models represent contributions from other sciences.

Elements of technology can be inserted into the production functions used. In early models very simple production functions were used, assuming proportionality between changes in volume of production and in labour force, which for short-term changes is adequate.

In later models, used for long-term development, a fixed capital-output ratio was used, sometimes for an economy as a whole, sometimes for individual sectors of the economy. In more refined models, substitution possibilities between capital and labour were introduced, first of all by the use of Cobb-Douglas production functions. Here, the volume of production is assumed to show a constant elasticity vis-à-vis the inputs of labour and capital. Recently, various types of labour have been introduced.

Elements of psychology have always been used in economics, but for a long time in a very primitive way, where only consumption of goods and services, during various periods, were supposed to determine welfare. More recently, other phenomena were added, such as the number of years of schooling received and the number of years of schooling required for the job chosen.

Sociological elements have been introduced into the models dealing with population increase, albeit for the time being in a primitive way.

This means that socio-economic models can act as a framework within which all the aspects relevant to the problem to be solved can be given their proper place. The model used by Meadows et al.[2] contains many examples of such an integration. Since its main purpose was to show the effects of population and production growth, pollution, and the exhaustion of some natural resources on the future well-being of mankind, extensive attention was given to the possibilities of increasing food production, implying geological and agronomic relationships, and to the feedbacks of pollution on capital allocation and population growth, implying new technological knowledge and medical relations between pollution and health. In comparison to Meadows' model, the socio-economic aspects of Kahn and Wiener's[3] model are primitive — it mainly consists of extrapolations — but its technological aspects have been much more emphasized. Verdoorn and Van den Beld[4] have been more sophisticated with regard to the production function used.

The models needed for today's main problems must contain many more extra-economic variates than has been customary so far, because of the 'limits to growth' recently detected, because the urgency of reducing mass poverty in developing countries is still not sufficiently understood, and because of the profound cultural and ethical changes pervading human society: let me mention only the increased value attached to national independence, to participation of employees in decision-making at various levels, etc.

Essential features of models are that — in contradistinction to verbal presentations — they 'administer', in a much more explicit and conscious way, the 'mechanism' (or 'organism', if one prefers) of society. This administration consists of 'lists' of variates, lists of equations or restrictions, and the particular mathematical — and in the end — numerical shape of these relations. Sometimes the complete system of equations can be represented by a matrix of coefficients — especially if all or many of the equations are linear. The solution of the problems posed depends, sometimes to a considerable degree, on the structure of a model's matrix, especially its ordering. A clear distinction should be made between two classes of problems, (i) forecasting or analytical and (ii) planning or policy problems.[5] Usually the former are supposed to be the problems of 'pure' science and the latter those of 'applied' science. Their difference is often less, however, than these terms suggest. In many cases the same model can be used for both, the difference only being which of the variates or variables are considered as given and which as unknown. In planning or policy problems the targets are given and the policy tools or instruments unknown; in forecasting or analytical problems it is the other way round. For several classes of models the solution of the planning or policy problem is simpler than that of the analytical problem, since the 'core' variates, that is, those which determine the main structure of the mechanism, are often among the target variables.

3. Principles of an efficient division of labour, I: A number of alternative models

Part of efficient scientific work consists of trying out different visions. This is already true because of differences in relevance as judged by different scientists or politicians. Thus, the problem of pollution may be treated by estimating the existing extent of pollution occurring with the processes now in use or by estimating the cost of avoiding it by changing processes. The former approach is closer to the analytical, the latter to the policy approach.

Another example of a difference of vision is the choice between macro and micro models. In economics there are well-known examples of macro models being more appropriate to bring out the essence of some problem than micro models. This is true for understanding the essence of balance of payment troubles, or for understanding the consequences of the existence of non-tradables, that is, products which cannot be imported or exported. If a micro model is necessary, difference of opinion may exist about which grouping of sectors is the best. For the problem of the best division of labour among rich and poor countries, some authors prefer a distinction between labour-intensive and capital-intensive industries, whereas others try to distinguish between less and more 'sophisticated' production processes.

For problems of environmental policies some authors have used world-wide models (Meadows) and others models for one region (Muller and Pelupessy;[6] Muller also dealt with the Meadows model.[7])

Education policy may be based on the target of maximum total production or on the target of less inequality in incomes; the two approaches again require different models. In a general way, planning models may differ because in one a limited number of policy instruments is admitted as feasible, whereas in another it is assumed that detailed intervention is feasible (mixed vs centrally planned societies).

Often, as a preparation for a general model of an economy, or a national society, models will be constructed for well-defined parts or aspects of the policy to be planned. Thus, the education sector has only been added to a purely production model after the need for future manpower of some particular types had become evident; recently, the increased interest in income distribution has induced me to investigate, with the aid of partial models on that subject, what factors seem to be relevant for the reduction of inequality in incomes. Depending on the outcome the general model can be extended in different ways. Similarly, partial models for industry complexes, for the earth's capacity to produce food, for various alternative future sources of energy, and for climatic consequences of pollution by carbon dioxide are being studied simultaneously by different persons or groups of persons.

4. *Principles of an efficient division of labour, II: Construction of a single model and the ensuing division of labour*

The main principle of an efficient division of labour for the construction of a single model is that a natural division of tasks rests on the existence of a number of separate equations or relations, and possibly restrictions. Many of such relations or restrictions will clearly belong to a single scientific area. Production functions, already given some attention in Section 2, are the realm of technologists (industrial, mining, agricultural, etc.). So are the particular forms of them, known as input-output or interindustry deliveries equations. Demand by consumers can be described by economists (sometimes especially market analysts) and sociologists. Nutrition and health restrictions can be dealt with by the corresponding medical experts.

In this way, a considerable number of tasks can be defined and distributed among individual institutes or working groups. A good example in the field of econometrics is to be found in what is known as the Brookings Quarterly Econometric Model of the United States. This model in its more elaborate form was supposed to contain 300 to 400 equations. In a progress report published in 1965 the main contributions made by several of the econometricians involved have been briefly described and this description comes close to the sort of division of labour just suggested.

On top of the series of tasks linked with the tentative formulation and testing of the individual equations, a central task consists of both an initial and a final phase of the work. The initial phase is the decision on the provisional list of variables, implying the choice of the degree of decomposition of the model. The final phase consists of the joint estimation of sets of equations or all the equations, depending on the structure of the coefficient matrix.

After an initial agreement on the provisional set-up, each group can concentrate on its set of equations. For a good timing of the project it is desirable that they should be ready at about the same time. This can be furthered by an appropriate staffing, that is, for each group a number of participants proportional to the estimated size of the task. Of course such an estimate cannot be very accurate and may have to be adapted from time to time. Since there have to be full meetings of all involved at regular intervals, in which progress reports can be discussed, the possibility for such adaptations of staffing exists.

The central group or institute — presumably with a relatively high number of econometricians — will have its second main task at the end of the operation. It must replace the provisional individual estimates of each relation by a simultaneous estimation, usually yielding changes in coefficients, and it will have to solve the problem, whether a forecasting or a planning problem, mainly a computer exercise. The solutions found will have to be discussed at the full meeting of participants and, after possible changes, will have to be written down in non-technical language. In this form it is appropriate for discussion in a meeting of political experts and other 'generalists'. Some phases of the work may have to be repeated before 'final' results are obtained. Of course, nothing in scientific work is really final, but there are healthy limits to be taken care of.

Depending on the structure of the model, sub-centres will be useful.[9] Thus, a number of relations containing the same variables, may all refer to the same discipline and may almost represent a submodel — almost, since a few variables may express the links with other parts of the model. Clearly, a sub-centre may be a useful coordinator at a lower level, meaning more freedom for the workers involved and less loss of time in coordinating discussions, which are not always a positive element.

5. *Some examples of possible cooperation at global level*

The preceding suggestions imply that for the construction and solution of one model among the alternatives considered useful a group of institutes cooperates, each of them in one of the fields needed. These institutes must be scientific institutes and not administrative or political bodies. For another version of, say, the Meadows Report, taking into account the existence of several regions with different average incomes, at least the following disciplines will have to participate in the project: demography, biology, agronomy, geology, physics, chemistry, various branches of technology, meteorology, sociology, economics, political science.

Since the cooperation is supposed to be temporary, its organizational structure should not be too heavy. One liaison officer in each institute should be informed about every contact taken up between the cooperating institutes. They will not, as a rule, be the representatives spoken of before, who together form the 'full meeting': the liaison officer can be a more administratively oriented staff member. As suggested before, some 'systems analysis' (to follow today's vogue) will be needed in order to have the results from each institute at about the same time. If, inside one of the institutes, problems taking a long time and others requiring less time have to be dealt with, the persons in charge of the long-term problems should not be bothered with a responsibility for the short-run contributions. Similarly — and this is relevant to the question as to what role the United Nations specialized agencies could play in large research projects — research workers of high quality should not be bothered with important administrative burdens.

In a way, a somewhat related pattern of work was used in the preparation of the Strategy for the Second United Nations Development Decade. To be sure, the participants in the meetings of the U.N. Development Planning Committee were not free from administrative duties; but all of them were experts in the particular field they represented. Thus, all the specialized agencies of the U.N. family were represented by staff members actively engaged in the field of development; the same applied to the representatives of the regional commissions, whether of the United Nations or of regional organizations independent of the U.N. (OECD, EEC, CMEA); it also applied, of course, to the representatives of the regional research and training institutes. The Centre for Development Planning, Projections and Policies of the Department of Economic and Social Affairs of the United Nations Secretariat acted not only as the secretariat of the Committee, but also as the 'centre' in the sense of this paper.

Nevertheless, there are also important differences between this operation and what is the subject of this paper. As already stated, this paper deals with full-time research workers and institutes, whereas the organizations involved in the preparation of the Strategy for the Second Development Decade have important other tasks in addition.

6. Some examples of inefficient methods

For the sake of clarity it is useful to add to the set of principles set out in the preceding sections some examples of what should be avoided in any set-up of (temporary) cooperation between research institutes. Most of what should be avoided is well known. Thus, duplication of routine inquiries or coordination activities should be avoided. In contrast, some duplication of pure thinking is rewarding as it may produce the 'choc des opinions (dont) jaillit la vérité'. Another closely related inefficient activity is too much or too lengthy summarizing of what others have been doing. A clear example of it is to be found in what has so far been done by a number of publishers in the field of regional planning.

It seems superfluous also to mention here, as an inefficient activity, the treatment of irrelevant problems. Unfortunately the warning is not superfluous. As irrelevant in my own field of economics I consider such research as the short-term prediction of share prices, purely an instrument for speculation on the stock exchange, which definitely does not satisfy a pressing need of mankind. Important portions of technological research have also been, in my opinion, of little relevance to the solution of the world's main problems; for instance, research to improve coffee substitutes.

A final example of irrelevant research is, up to a point, criticism of the Meadows Report for omissions or errors, without a full test of the quantitative significance of the criticism with the aid of a complete model. It is one thing to point out a shortcoming, but it is quite a different thing to estimate the impact of the shortcoming on the final answers of the model. Therefore only criticisms arrived at with the aid of a complete model are really relevant.[10]

NOTES

1 An interesting survey of the performance of econometric models for the United States is given by Gary Fromm and Lawrence R. Klein in 'A Comparison of Eleven Econometric Models of the United States', *The Amer. Econ. Review, Papers and Proceedings*, May 1973, p. 385.

2 Donella H. Meadows, Dennis L. Meadows, Jørgen Randers and William W. Behrens III, *The Limits to Growth*, New York 1972.

3 Herman Kahn and Anthony J. Wiener, *The Year 2000*, New York 1967.

4 C. A. van den Beld, *De Nederlandse economie in 2000*, Haarlem 1967. (In Dutch), quoted in H. Janne (ed.), *The Future is To-Morrow*, European Cultural Foundation, The Hague 1972, p. 303.

5 J. Tinbergen, 'Two Approaches to the Future: Planning vs Forecasting', in: *Essays in Honour of Giuseppe Ugo Papi*, Padova 1973, pp. 333 ff.

6 F. Muller and W. Pelupessy, 'Economische waardering van de schaarse lucht in Rijnmond', *Economisch Statistische Berichten* 56 (1971), p. 203 (in Dutch).

7 F. Muller, 'Maatregelen van economische politiek in het wereldmodel van de Club van Rome' (Measures of economic policy in the world model of the Club of Rome), *Economisch Statistische Berichten* 58, 1973, p. 640 (in Dutch).

8 J. S. Duesenberry, G. Fromm, L. R. Klein and E. Kuh, *The Brookings Quarterly Econometric Model of the United States*, Amsterdam 1965.

9 Clear examples occurring in Hungarian socio-economic planning can be found in J. Kornai, *Mathematical Planning of Structural Decisions*, Amsterdam 1967.

10 This, then, applies to the larger part of the critique of the Meadows Report. It does not imply, of course, that the Meadows Report is 'correct' or 'accurate'.

ARE SCIENTISTS AND TECHNOLOGISTS PREPARED FOR INTERNATIONAL COORDINATION?

Sam Nilsson, International Federation of Institutes for Advanced Study (IFIAS), Stockholm

Dr Gresford gives us in his abstract, distributed in advance to this symposium, his views on the past, present, and future role of the UN 'family' regarding coordination and use of Science and Technology in coping with international problems.

He sees a need *now* for the UN system to adapt its organizational structure and methods to more flexible and non-structured management procedures for mobilizing the world's scientific and technological talents in international cooperation.

He sees a need for a clearly articulated 'World Science Policy'.

Just a few days ago Lord Ritchie-Calder said at the San Fransisco Press Club that we are in a desperate need of a 'World Science Policy'. He feels that 'mankind faces a scientific crisis' which is caused in part by the perfection of the crash programs. 'Scientists have learned to pool their resources and telescope 100 years of research into less than a decade', he said. Each revolution had its good and bad consequences. Antibiotics, while able to save countless lives, were unleashed on less developed nations after the war. Infant mortality dropped, populations exploded, and poverty resulted. 'The tragedy of it' — he said — is that there is no internationally accepted set of guidelines for the application of scientific knowledge. *'We have too much knowledge, not enough wisdom'*, Lord Ritichie-Calder concluded.

The world science policy, whatever form it should take and whatever institutions might be created to implement it, 'would promote the use of scientists in decision-making bodies, and would function to prevent the misuse of knowledge'.

In a way we have a world science policy already, however. But it has been developed by the peers of the scientific establishment themselves. There have been no socially normative elements working. This is what the politicians and society at large are now demanding.

Some time ago a book appeared which is probably the most articulate summary of the attitudes of many young people toward science. Theodore Roszak in his book *The Making of a Counter Culture*, accuses all science of being an antihuman activity, the consequence of which is alienation — through its impact we become strangers to ourselves and we cannot tolerate our very existence, Roszak concludes.

For thousands of years man was trying to master nature to make for himself a better life. But when at long last he mastered nature, he lost interest in life itself. This is what is happening to the young generation: their feeling is that first of all one should get rid of that natural curiosity which underlies science.

There is little doubt, however, that the curiosity of man in general and of scientists in particular has deep biological roots, for curiosity is found in all the animal world.

But, the young generation complains that science has led to a hypertrophy of curiosity — scientists have a pathological curiosity which satisfies only themselves in their own narrow fields of specialization and for this satisfaction they are ready to sacrifice the life of mankind. Hence the salvation of mankind lies in anti-intellectualism and anti-scientism.

Man's confidence in his power to control his world is certainly at a low ebb. Technology is seen as a dangerous ally, and progress is suspect. As one of the most critical disturbances is seen the threat to an old and honored dichotomy. In the theo-centric world of the Middle Ages, man lived in a holistic universe, with heaven above and earth below embraced in one divine economy.

But the aggressive humanism of the Renaissance and the mechanistic visions of the scientific revolution shattered that unified cosmos. A religious man, but also a rationalist, René Descartes contended that man could demonstrate truth only about a world he could measure. The world of spirit was beyond such measurement, a matter of faith and intuition, not truth. Descartes became a self-fulfilling prophet. The spiritual world was left to philosophers and divines, many of whom shared the Cartesian bias that theirs was an ephemeral discipline. The physical world became the domain of Western Science, though man sometimes seemed less the master of that world than its mechanic.

Now, with a sense that materialism is bankrupt, many men are challenging the dualistic vision. One reason for their challenge may be the new concern for the environment. Another, and related reason, is the notion of 'only one earth' with limited resources to feed, shelter, and educate a steadily increasing population.

None of these ideas are as yet majority views in the Western World, and they may never be. The reason why I have taken your time to discuss them briefly here, is that I am convinced that they are going to affect the national and international science policies and our ability to mobilize scientists and technologists for attacking the burning world issues.

What can be done?

In my opinion, the cure for the excesses of anti-scientism must lie in greater circumspection on part of the scientists. Granted that the future repercussions of scientific discoveries cannot be predicted with accuracy, scientists could still be more reflective about these matters — and their reflectiveness should be institutionalized and continuous instead of intermittent and apocalyptic. They must guard themselves against their own self-serving propensities. Scientists must avoid striking Promethean poses. They must learn to say 'no' in a discriminating way to all the opportunities which knowledge and research offer them. They must learn that 'more' is not necessarily better. Above all they must not yield to the temptations of the prophetic role.

Let me again refer to Dr Gresford's abstract to this symposium. He says that a policy for the UN family must take account of the following considerations among several others:

> The growth of science has profoundly influenced not only individuals and nations but mankind as a whole and its future. To be in a position to influence the future by political action it is essential to be able to define the options which are open and what the impact of science and technology will be ...
>
> Tools for this are starting to be developed. As a global approach becomes not only possible but necessary, the problems of the future must become of increasing concern to the UN family, which must encourage the development and application of means of planning on a global scale.

I agree entirely with these viewpoints. But how could we reach these goals? Richard Gardner and myself have seen the attempts by UNITAR to establish a 'Council for the Future' which would serve as the focal point for probing the future options in areas of great concern to the UN family and help to advise on the necessary integrated approaches on issues which need the involvement of the best intellectual resources, wherever they are in the world, in a transdisciplinary and transnational way.

This initiative has, as far as I know, the moral support of the prominent trustees of UNITAR as well as of the UN Secretary-General.

Dr Gardner and I participated in a preparatory and rather constructive discussion on this proposal in London in December 1972.

Since then I have heard nothing. I regret this because I saw it as a first promising step toward a vital role by the UN family and in the direction which Dr Gresford sees as necessary. It is also a pity because I believe that much could already have been achieved by beginning with one seriously devoted person to map out the keenness, ability, and willingness to assist of the world intellectual community. For a very modest cost not only this would have been achieved but also, as a by-product, a tentative list could have been drawn up of important issues to begin with. When I was asked in October 1971 to make a detailed feasibility study of the creation of a network of research institutions in different disciplines I travelled around the world to some 25 research institutes. I also had the privilege and opportunity of meeting a great number of individuals at different levels in the decision-making echelon. I came home with a wide spectrum of impressions and suggestions on which I based my recommendations to establish the International Federation of Institutes for Advanced Study, IFIAS.

Two points made an especially deep impression on my memory because they were reinforced as I met more and more people. I think they are interesting enough to mention at this symposium;

(i) Responsible scientists and technologists in the less developed countries are very much worried that the decision-makers will take science and technology as the only recipe for development. They are much concerned about the necessity of introducing science and technology only if it takes into account the social and cultural needs of man and his values.

(ii) The present university system will not be able to respond constructively and quickly enough to the new challenges either from the anti-intellectualist or from the world 'problematique' as spelled out in the current debate on growth. New flexible structures and procedures are needed which make it possible to mobilize the world intellectual community on an 'ad hoc' basis as the problems emerge.

The International Federation of Institutes for Advanced Study (IFIAS)

The thoughts and ideas which led up to the formation of IFIAS began at a Nobel Symposium in Stockholm in 1969 called 'The Place of Value in a World of Facts'.[1]

IFIAS is one of a number of emerging enterprises which reflect the need for new mechanisms and insights to help society cope with an increasingly complex, rapidly changing, and interdependent world. It was established in October 1972 under the auspices of the Nobel and Rockefeller Foundations. It is expected that IFIAS will provide useful 'pilot models' for such mechanisms as may be adopted by others, independently or in cooperation with IFIAS, for instance the emerging UN University. After having read the latest report by the committee under Dr Andrew Cordier, now working on the UN University, I can see, for instance, that the role meant for the UNITAR's 'Council for the Future' mentioned above may be adopted as one of the first tasks of a UN University.

IFIAS is a non-governmental, non-profit-making, and highly flexible organization designed to help build bridges between the natural sciences and those concerned with the deep dimensions of social, cultural, and humanistic aspects of man and his needs.

The uniqueness of IFIAS as an international federation derives from its dedication to inter-institutional cooperation of a transdisciplinary and transnational character.

By 'transdisciplinary', IFIAS affirms that its efforts in international cooperation transcend disciplinary bonds, aiming not merely to join physicists to chemists or mathematicians to economists, but to bring to its programs and projects those aspects which are of particular concern to the ethical, social, and humanistic consequences of various lines of research and analyses, and which pay attention to the assessment of policy alternatives facing decision-makers in respect of new knowledge and its uses. In order to ensure such relevance it is expected that decision-makers will be enlisted in the activities at an early stage of the work.

Thus you may say that IFIAS is an attempt *both* to mobilize systematically, but informally, the best talents in the world, without regard to disciplinary or geographical borders, to tackle specific problems, *and* to build a new type of intellectual community for 'continuous awareness' of world problems.

This is clearly reflected in the three principal objectives of IFIAS:
(1) Joint transnational and transdisciplinary research and analyses involving several of its Member Institutes as well as other institutions, scholars, and experts who share its interests and represent the highest standards of knowledge and proficiency in order to approach problems which require fresh reviews, assessments, and insight not being provided adequately through traditional means.
(2) Exchanges among its members, both in industrialized and less developed areas of the world of faculties, scholars, and postdoctoral students to provide experiences not readily available elsewhere.
(3) The building of a new type of community of joint interests and

programs through a continuous and orderly exchange of the plans of the Member Institutes, as well as the collective and comprehensive examination of new ideas, concepts, materials, and evaluations of the long-term implications of the consequences of their work.

IFIAS has been established with a minimum of structure but with strict criteria for the selection of its programs and projects. It will consciously attempt to compensate for certain of the obstacles facing existing governmental bodies, whether international or non-governmental, which are built around a special discipline or a sector and which have somewhat inflexible organizations and procedures.

Political considerations often make it difficult to assess objectively the wide range of policy questions which characterize many of the world problems.

Membership structure

IFIAS Member Institutes represent at present ten disciplines and some fifteen countries in North and Latin America, Europe, Asia, Australia, and Africa.

Aspen Institue for Humanistic Studies, New York, USA

Athens Center of Ekistics, Athens, Greece

Center for Theoretical Studies, University of Miami, Coral Gables, Flo., USA

El Colegio de Mexico, Mexico City, Mexico

Dept. of Cell Research and Genetics, Medical Nobel Institute, Karolinska Institutet, Stockholm, Sweden

Instituto de Biofísica, Rio de Janeiro, Brazil

International Centre for Theoretical Physics, Trieste, Italy

The International Centre of Insect Physiology and Ecology, Nairobi, Kenya

The International Rice Research Institute, Manila, the Philippines

The Japan Economic Research Center, Tokyo, Japan

Johnson Research Foundation, Philadelphia, Penn., USA

Mathematics Institute, University of Warwick, Coventry, UK

Niels Bohr Institutet of Physics, Copenhagen, Denmark

The Pasteur Institute, Paris, France

Tata Institute of Fundamental Research, Bombay, India

University Corporation for Atmospheric Research, Boulder, Colo., USA

The Walter and Eliza Hall Institute of Medical Research, Victoria, Australia

The Weizmann Institute of Science, Rehovot, Israel

Woods Hole Oceanographic Institution, Woods Hole, Mass., USA

To ensure a balanced geographical and disciplinary distribution but at the same time keep the group of institutes to a manageable size it has been decided to keep the number below thirty during the initial period of three to five years. IFIAS is still weak in social sciences and the humanities and in members from less developed countries.

In this connection it should be emphasized, however, that IFIAS is not a closed group of elitist institutions. Each of the Member Institutes has agreed to fulfill its duty to identify in its own field such other individuals or institutions which may contribute and participate actively in any of the IFIAS activities and to help enlarge the intellectual community. We also have some twenty Special Advisers serving in their personal capacity with advice and suggestions in matters which are generally not in the realm of a special institute. Hereby, our real and potential network of contacts over the world has become very large and multidimensional.

The Board of IFIAS includes all the Directors of the Member Institutes, who are in a position to influence quickly and directly the deployment of their individual institute resources to the new common efforts. The first Chairman of the Board is Dr Nils K. Ståhle.

By common consent the Executive Secretariat was placed in Stockholm, at least for the initial period. It is small, only four persons, and builds its activities and initiatives mostly on personal contacts, to the least possible degree on paper communication.

Projects and programs
At the founding meeting in Trieste in October, 1972, four projects and two programs were conditionally approved by the Board of Trustees for further screening under the strict procedures and criteria adopted by IFIAS.

These projects and programs were proposed by the Trustees, by Special Advisers, Institute Scientists, or persons outside the IFIAS member structure.

The projects are:
(1) Water resources and strategies for management
   This complex subject, which is under study by specialists in many parts of the world, demands comprehension, decision-making, and the initiation of transnational and transdisciplinary work. Its study involves questions of supply and demand, conservation and renewal, food, health and recreation, and countless conflicts of interests among users of one of the more vital of our environmental resources and one which is shrinking dramatically in many parts of the world.

(2) Human settlements: understanding their nature and guiding their development for the benefit of Man.

One of the most pervasive problems of all societies is an understanding of the elements which determine the *quality of life* in human settlements and the things which have and can be done to improve man's life in human settlements where nearly all mankind lives. This problem is being tackled in many places, but IFIAS feels justified in exploring whether its array of resources and its opportunities for special linkages among a variety *of disciplines might lead to an integrated* project which might give a new insight in this complex field. Thus steps are being taken to explore the potential design of and participants in an IFIAS Special Project.

(3) Social and ethical implications of enzyme technology.

Breakthroughs seem to be appearing which may open up a wide range of new applications of enzyme technology from medicine to protein synthesis and to fuel cells for solar energy utilization. *Some of the potential applications may have profound social, ethical, and economic implications.* Special expertise in enzyme science and technology is possessed by certain IFIAS members and there is interest in exploring the implications of various consequences by IFIAS members from economics and social sciences. As a first step in exploring the design and justification of an IFIAS Special Project, IFIAS has designated one of its advisers to bring together, for potential future IFIAS support and endorsement, the many threads of such a project.

(4) The impact of climate changes on Man.

Some recent studies focused on man's impact on climate indicate that a projection of current trends may cause significant climate changes (rainfall, temperature, sunlight, seasonal distribution, etc.) in large areas of the world. When added to natural fluctuation the consequences could have profound effects on man's use of land and water. *Yet the social, economic, political, and cultural impact of climate on man has been studied very little and only in discipline fragments.* A study of the impact of climate on man has engaged several of the IFIAS institutes in different countries and it is expected that after further preparatory work an IFIAS Special Project involving cooperation of such institutes will be initiated.

The programs are:

(1) Implications of choices — energy and Man

IFIAS will convene a small panel of advisers to determine

whether the many current studies of energy sources provide an adequate assessment of the social, ethical, and humanistic implications of the decisions societies may make concerning their principal sources of energy for the future. If the panel concludes that a study of such implications of choices is needed and can recommend a qualified individual, IFIAS may commission that individual to make such a study, arrange critiques of the resulting Report to accompany it, and bring the product to wide public attention.

(2) Schistosomiasis — program for a case study.

While the bio-medical aspects of schistosomiasis, its immunology, and the effects of various molluscocides on the snails have been and are being extensively studied, and are fairly well understood, there has been, to our knowledge, no adequate in-depth study of the simultaneous evolution and complex interplay of the behavioral, educational, social, cultural, economical, engineering, and medical factors which affect this and other communicable tropical diseases and their prevalence. The recent Nobel Workshop in Stockholm, initiated by IFIAS, confirmed this. The participants representing agriculture, epidemiology, economics, sanitary engineering, ecology, medicine, and management worked out a concrete plan for an intensive study over six years of the events that occur when a water development scheme is implemented in a 'schisto'-region.

The Workshop participants recommended that IFIAS, with its multidisciplinary composition, may be the ideal setting for an initiative to launch such a program with the World Bank and other concerned bodies.

Obstacles and challenges to IFIAS

Many of the obstacles which are met in any effort of international coordination of scientists and technologists are, of course, also met by IFIAS. It is evident that a mobilization of intellectuals in 'transdisciplinary and transnational activities' must be even more difficult than bringing together a group of, for instance, water resources experts.

Most of our member institutes and other international organizations have limited experience of truly transdisciplinary work. This was, in fact, one of the principal reasons why IFIAS was formed. And here I think it is much easier to work with existing research institutes with experience in dealing with complex issues in an international environment than to build up new institutions.

Since IFIAS will deal mostly with issues of global and long-range importance it may be difficult to *formulate policy alternatives* which are strongly enough anchored in the modern world of perception of consumers and decision-makers. The policy recommendations may therefore be looked upon as interesting curiosities with no effect on the actions. Many politicians think (and sometimes rightly) that conspiracies are afoot to control the changes in society through elite groups. Without arrogating from the 'elitist' position IFIAS will try to impose its will and recommendations on consumers and decision-makers. In this endeavor our Special Advisers play an important role.

Most national, company, and institute research budgets are of short-range (1—3 years). Few researchers at universities, companies, and special institutions are involved in assessments and analyses which have a bearing on the long-range (10—30 years) social, economic, and cultural transformations of society.

There is no particular merit in the present academic system whereby an individual researcher or team devotes full-time work to long-term evaluations of world issues and even tries to present alternative choices among the options available. Long-term assessments can easily result in conclusions which appear platitudinous and the credibility is spoiled.

Allow me to conclude by referring to what Finn Sollie says in his abstract to this symposium:

> The coordination in the field of natural science, technology, social sciences and the humanities, which is in one sense an organizational problem is in many respects a political problem. Neither problem, or rather cluster of problems, has an easy solution and this may call for a step-by-step approach.
>
> No complete system for full-scale international coordination can be envisaged today. *By concentrating on a few international problems it may nevertheless be possible both to achieve effective coordination and to gain experience for future development.*

IFIAS is one such attempt to gain experience both with transdisciplinary projects and to build, step-by-step, a new type of world intellectual community.

Finally I would like to emphasize that I do not think that there is one unique way to effective and constructive coordination in science and technology. What I know, however, is that we must start preparing *in advance*. Will scientists and technologists then be prepared for international coordination and cooperation? After one year's experience with IFIAS I am inclined to say yes. But it is difficult; it will take time and a rather special type of approach and leadership, of which we have limited experience.

NOTES
1 The Place of Value in a World of Facts. *Proceedings of the Fourteenth Nobel Symposium,* Stockholm, September 15—20, 1969; Edited by Arne Tiselius and Sam Nilsson; Almqvist & Wiksell Förlag AB, Stockholm, 1970.

THE ROLE OF THE UNITED NATIONS FAMILY IN FURTHERING SCIENCE AND TECHNOLOGY THROUGH INTERNATIONAL COOPERATION

Guy B. Gresford, United Nations, New York

Since the sudden upsurge of interest in the environment appeared a few years ago, it has become fashionable to speak and write about Spaceship Earth 'with its living cargo sustained by a unitary, limited and vulnerable life support system'.[1] This concept is of immense value in enabling us to think in terms of a 'systems approach' and underlines the need for a global science policy. It may perhaps help to provide a political incentive towards the achievement of the brotherhood of man — sought so long by philosophers and scholars — and the objectives of the United Nations. But it is only too apparent that the crew of Spaceship Earth is not a happy or united one. The members differ widely in their background, training and experience; there is a very wide and unjust variation in their ranks and their rewards; they are not unanimous in what they hold to be the objectives of their mission and they do not acknowledge any one union or commander.

One common thread, however, which runs through the beliefs of all members of the crew of Spaceship Earth is a belief in the vital role of science and technology in sustaining and navigating the spaceship (though there is a wide variation of views as to whither the ship should journey). In the more advanced parts of the spaceship, i.e. in the developed countries, science and technology have been immensely successful in many areas of importance to human well-being. The faith shown in them is evident from the fact that 98 % of the world's research and development is carried out in advanced countries.[2] Only in recent years has some questioning arisen as to the real degree of this success. As has been pointed out recently in an OECD report,[3] '...it is realized that the immense social benefits that have flowed from science and technology are sometimes accompanied by social disbenefits. Thus, policies concerned with science and technology in the next decade will have to take into account, much more explicitly than in the past, the benefits and disbenefits, actual and potential, that may result from the application of science or the development of technology'. Despite fears in some advanced countries that the anti-science movement may be gaining significant strength, this questioning must at least result in a more critical analysis of national science policies and a reordering of priorities — both, it would appear, desirable developments.

In the developing world, however, the situation is very different. Parenthetically, one should emphasize that the term 'developing world' covers an immense spectrum ranging from those countries with a highly sophisticated science establishment to those with almost zero scientific activity. Compare, for example, India and Chad. Here the potential contributions of science and technology are disappointingly slow in being realized. In his address to the 1963 United Nations Conference on the Application of Science and Technology for the Benefit of the Less Developed Areas, U Thant pointed out the need for the conference to 'focus the attention of the scientific world on one of the most urgent needs of contemporary society, the need to combat poverty, chronic disease and illiteracy, the need to raise more than two-thirds of the world population to a condition compatible with human dignity'.[4] He went on to emphasize the need for new research to deal successfully with some of the most pressing problems of new nations, and the question of how science and technology can be absorbed effectively by developing countries. In the ten years that have elapsed since that conference, there has been limited achievement, although the dimensions of the problem have grown wider more quickly than the efforts to solve it. A significant measure of the situation is the corollary of the figure quoted for the amount of research and development undertaken by the advanced world, viz. only 2 % of the world's research and development is carried out in developing countries.

It is against this background — in the developed world a growing realization of the need to take into account the social as well as economic results of the application of science and technology and in the developing countries the vital urgency of employing the tools of science and technology more effectively — that the role of the United Nations family in furthering science and technology through international cooperation must be considered.

The different organizations which now constitute the United Nations family of specialized agencies have been established on a pragmatic basis over a considerable period to provide for international cooperation to meet needs in specific fields. These organizations are independent entities, each with its own governing body elected by Member States. They share, however, a number of common procedures; they are all involved in providing technical aid to developing countries, and their activities are coordinated through the United Nations Economic and Social Council. Most of them are, to a greater

42

or lesser extent, concerned with facilitating international cooperation in science and technology.

Some of the agencies have been in existence for many years and owe their existence to the need for international action in establishing standards, or collecting and analyzing data necessary for furthering the application of science and technology in their respective fields. The International Telecommunication Union, which recently celebrated its centenary, has as its objective the harmonization of national actions for the improvement and rational use of telecommunications and for promoting the development and most efficient operation of technical facilities. The World Meteorological Organization, which descends from a conference held as long ago as 1853, has the mandate of coordinating, standardizing the improving world meteorological activities and encouraging an efficient exchange of meteorological information between countries in the aid of human activities. Other agencies are concerned with the application of science and technology for the improvement of the human condition — both in developed and developing countries — through international cooperation. The Food and Agriculture Organization of the United Nations (established in 1945) is concerned with raising levels of nutrition and standards of living, with the improvement of production and distribution of agricultural products and the betterment of the condition of rural populations. The objective of the World Health Organization (established in 1946) is 'the attainment by all peoples of the highest possible level of health', health being defined as 'a state of complete physical, mental and social well-being, and not merely the absence of disease or infirmity'.

The United Nations Educational, Scientific and Cultural Organization, also established in 1946, has the objective, as far as science is concerned, of stimulating and assisting the growth and well-being of science itself. It gives institutional expression to the traditional international nature of science, and its integration with education and culture.

The International Atomic Energy Agency was established in response to the need for an international approach to the political problems raised by the explosive growth and dramatic success of nuclear science in the period starting with the Second World War.

The most recent body to be added to the United Nations family — it is a part of the United Nations itself — is the United Nations Environment Program, established as a consequence of the 1972 United Nations Conference on the Human Environment, to fill the urgent need for international machinery to deal with regional and global problems of the environment. In the third world these problems are largely the consequence of poverty and underdevelopment; in the advanced countries they arise in large measure from the impact of uncontrolled application of science and technology. The United Nations Environment Programme therefore differs from many of the other components of the United Nations system in that its interests are not confined to any one sector of human activity but range 'across the board'. It might be pointed out that in a similar way science and technology, which do not represent any one sector but rather may be considered as tools for the improvement of human well-being, thus permeate the activities of almost all the units which make up the United Nations family.

Considering the fact that the United Nations was established as an aftermath of the Second World War, an event which emphasized dramatically the power of science and technology, it may appear strange that no mention of science or technology appears in its Charter. The Charter, however, is concerned in the broad sense with ends rather than means, and it is the various specialized agencies that have provided means for employing science and technology to meet the political and social ends of the system. It is becoming more and more evident, however, that the direct influence of science and technology as a means on the affairs of the United Nations is constantly increasing.

The problems of the developing world are at the heart of the United Nations debate, and these are problems in the solution of which science and technology must play a key role. In addition to the urgent need for responding to these problems, however, the United Nations, as the most nearly universal intergovernmental political organization, must also increasingly respond to those questions of growing urgency in which scientific and technological considerations interact with political ones. The list of such specific questions is constantly being enlarged; as examples, one may quote those relating to outer space, the sea-bed, population, the transfer of technology, the energy crisis, or the problems of natural resources.

At the national level, in developed countries, the 'social function of science', as articulated by Bernal in 1939 is no longer an issue for debate, and the need for a science policy, though its exact content or how it should be achieved is still a matter for argument, is widely accepted. In developing countries, the concept of science policy as a component of economic planning is also gaining ground, influenced to a large degree by the science policy program of UNESCO and the activities of other United Nations agencies. The United Nations Advisory Committee on the Application of Science and Technology has made the need for science policy a major element in its World Plan of

Action for the Application of Science and Technology to Development.[5] The United Nations system at present provides an arbitrary framework for international cooperation at the governmental level, but such an international science policy is lacking. Until such a policy is formulated and accepted, the full potentialities of the role of the United Nations family in furthering science and technology through global cooperation must remain unfulfilled.

In considering a science policy for the United Nations family, there are a number of areas which should be emphasized.

Imbalance in science and technology between developed and developing countries

The great imbalance between the science and technology of developed and developing countries has been pointed out earlier. The programs of all members of the United Nations family are in effect directed to the building up of indigenous science and technology in the developing countries. The work of the specialized agencies in their respective fields of competence aims at strengthening these activities and in assisting developing countries to establish cooperative links in science and technology with the developed world. The World Plan of Action for the Application of Science and Technology to Development, which was drawn up by the United Nations Advisory Committee on the Application of Science and Technology to Development in close collaboration with members of the United Nations family, is 'based on the conviction . . . that the more purposeful application of the powers of science and technology to development must be a matter of 'full international cooperation' and that the United Nations offers the natural framework for such international cooperation, although not necessarily the only one.'[5] The Strategy for the Second United Nations Development Decade adopted by the twenty-fifth General Assembly refers specifically to the question of international cooperation in science and technology for development. Concerted efforts are to be made by developing countries, 'with appropriate assistance from developed countries', to expand their capabilities in applying science and technology in development. 'Full international cooperation will be extended for the establishment, strengthening and promotion of scientific research and technological activities which have a bearing on the expansion and modernization of the economies of developing countries.'[6] The role of the United Nations family in furthering science and technology in this area is thus clearly envisaged; in addition, a special responsibility lies with the governments and with the scientific community of developed countries to ensure that these principles are carried out.

In much of the literature devoted to development, science and technology are coupled, without any attempt to define the boundaries between them. This is a subject for considerable argument and it would be inappropriate to discuss it here, but the importance of ensuring the cultivation of a vigorous indigenous *science* as well as building up technology in developing countries must be underlined. The need for this has been frequently emphasized; it has been well put in a recent paper by Haskins, who refers to 'the clear recognition of the paradox that, on the one hand, the basic motivations of science and the requirements for its healthy development are quite distinct from those of technology, yet that on the other a close and vital partnership must be built between the two; the formation and continuous cultivation of that partnership provide in combination a fundamental challenge to all the developing societies that are being caught up in the intense scientific-technological sweep of the world, and seek to survive in it'.[7] It is essential that developing countries, in building up their technology, should also ensure that they develop their science, which need not be a carbon copy of that in advanced countries, but should respond to their own conditions and needs.

Research on specific problems of developing countries
The wide quantitative disparity in the research and development efforts of developed and developing countries has already been mentioned. This is compounded, however, by the fact that some of the research effort of the developed countries — directed towards the solution of their own problems — is inimical to the interests of the developing countries. The intensive research devoted to synthetic materials, rather than to the improvement of natural products, on which many developing countries depend, is a case in point. The lack of attention by developed countries to the need for technologies appropriate to the conditions of developing countries may also be cited. The United Nations Advisory Committee on the Application of Science and Technology to Development has drawn attention to this matter in the World Plan of Action and has proposed quantitative targets of expenditure by developed countries on specific problems of developing countries. They are suggested in the expectation that developed countries will be willing to devote increasing and specified proportions of their own research and development expenditure to the development of knowledge and experience urgently needed for the solution of the specific problems of developing countries and, in addition, will be willing to undertake such research as part of their own programs, outside their direct aid programs. A panel of experts convened by the Secretary-General of the United Nations has sug-

gested some criteria for areas which could be dealt with under such targets.[8] These include:

— Areas in which there is a special need for new knowledge (as distinct from the adaptation of existing knowledge, best undertaken in the developing countries themselves);
— Areas and projects which need refined and sophisticated technological support of a kind at present only available in developed countries;
— Projects needing specialized scientists and technologists of a kind best available in developed countries;
— Projects of special global or common interest which will not be adequately reflected in the development plans, aid requests, and national expenditures of developing countries. Some of these are problems common to developed countries, e.g. marine pollution and human settlements.

The United Nations family, in view of its familiarity with many of these problem areas, can play a vital role in stimulating this type of international collaboration. The scientific community of the developed countries, collaborating with United Nations agencies, must itself play a leading part in such activities. The question is not simply one of the developed countries assisting the developing ones. There are numerous examples, particularly in such fields as agriculture, medicine and public health and the chemistry of natural products, in which the scientific and technological activities of developing countries are of benefit to other developing countries — or of great benefit to developed countries.

International needs

The need for an international science policy, as discussed, arises from the overriding urgency — both from the political and ethical points of view — of the problems of underdevelopment. The responsibility of the United Nations family in furthering science and technology to cope with these problems is widely accepted, and the discharge of such a role is basically controlled by the extent of the resources which governments make available. As has been pointed out, however, another set of issues arises — for the most part but not exclusively, in developed countries — from the uncontrolled application of science and technology. These issues include physical problems such as pollution and environmental degradation or the availability of natural resources, and also political problems arising from scientific and technological advances such as the control of nuclear weapons, sovereignty over the sea-bed or outer space, and the possibilities of climate modification. While such problems grew in the first instance from the

47

success of science and technology in developed countries, they rapidly became problems for the developing countries as well, and hence, because of their *international* nature, a matter of concern to the United Nations family.

In any consideration of international problems, the population question demands prominence. Population as a problem arose in part from the successful application of science and technology in the health field. The effects are seen mainly in developing countries, where efforts to overcome problems of underdevelopment are partially nullified by rising numbers of people. The matter is complex, and politically delicate, but it is one in which the interest and activities of the United Nations family are being increasingly welcomed. The organization of the United Nations World Population Conference in 1974 is an indication of the growing realization that the matter must receive international attention.

Such problems as these result in what Skolnikoff terms the international imperatives of technology. He points out that 'developments in science and technology, and the increasing application of technology, coupled with a rapidly growing population, in the next 10—20 years will necessitate a substantial expansion of the functions performed by international machinery'.[9] The United Nations family must bear a large part of the responsibility and indeed already does so. In Skolnikoff's analysis, the priority needs are to establish worldwide monitoring networks of environmental change, to develop analytical capabilities that are accepted as being impartial, to provide more extensive norm-creating, allocation, and rule-observance capabilities to meet the *institutional* requirements for dealing with environmental matters; to develop operational capabilities within the international machinery, and finally to develop an international institutional capability for the testing and evaluation of chemical agents used by men. The establishment of the United Nations Environment Program promises to go some distance towards meeting some of these needs for international cooperation, but many problems of coordination still remain, and the necessity of a truly global approach still awaits acceptance.

Projections of the future

Associated with the intense public discussion of recent years on problems of the environment has been a growing concern with the future — not seen in terms of a nation or a particular segment of society — but from the macro viewpoint of mankind as a whole. This concern is epitomized by the arguments arising from the publication of the Club of Rome study 'The Limits to Growth'. It also finds expression in the growing number of institutes and programs devoted to studies of the future, ranging from simple statistical projections of the demand and supply of raw materials to sophisticated systems studies of world trends. In all of these studies, science and technology — particularly technology — are vital elements because of their major roles in shaping the future, though it should not be assumed that continuous technical progress is inevitable. In drafting an international science policy, however, it must be understood that the quality of life of future generations depends largely on the wise deployment of scientific resources today. In Freeman's words, 'world R&D is in the nature of a global insurance policy'.[10]

Research and development, however, must be appropriate to global needs, and the policy directing it must aim not only at solving problems and meeting needs, but also at avoiding undesirable effects. The emerging techniques of technology assessment and technological forecasting promise to be of the greatest importance here, and they should constitute an important area for future activity in the United Nations family.

The search for knowledge and understanding
The classic function of natural science has been that of inquiry into natural phenomena in order to deepen our understanding of them. It is only in comparatively recent times that the link between science and technology has become close and that the need for basic scientific knowledge as a prerequisite for the development of technology has emerged. Participants in this symposium would, I believe — without going into the often rather sterile debate of pure versus applied research — support the view that science must be pursued for its own sake as well as for the technology which it may generate. Science has traditionally been international, and in recent times, along with other aspects of culture, has become an instrument of détente. But apart from cultural or political imperatives, there are technical reasons why science, to be effective, must become increasingly international. Many of the frontiers of knowledge facing such sciences as oceanography, seismology, meteorology, or other aspects of geophysics involve global problems which require international research. Some research has become so complex and costly that it is beyond the resources of any but the largest and wealthiest countries, not only in terms of financial resources but also in terms of trained manpower. The information problem and the need for adequate communication also make international collaboration a *sine qua non* for progress. Much of the activity of the United Nations family in the field of science and technology has arisen from these needs; its role is inherent

in its international composition. For the future development of science and technology, the role of the United Nations family in assisting international collaboration is a crucial one which must be exercised in the closest collaboration with the scientific community. (While the above remarks refer to the natural sciences, I believe they may also apply with increasing relevance to many activities in the social sciences field. In any event, science, in United Nations terms, should be considered as the German 'Wissenschaft'.)

Science and technology and human rights
As the year 1984 approaches, many of the situations envisaged by George Orwell in 1949 have already been realized or indeed surpassed. Electronic surveillance, the development of computer data banks, the development of chemicals which affect the brain and the possibilities of 'bioengineering' all are potential threats to human liberty and freedom, which the United Nations system is dedicated to protect. While, as Ritchie-Calder has pointed out, science itself is a human right — the inalienable (and irrepressible) right of natural curiosity — the erosion of human rights and incursions into personal and cultural privacy can happen by default, or be encouraged by a fascination with gadgets and ingenious methods.[11] This general problem of the possible effects of advances in science and technology on human rights is a very subtle one to which the United Nations has already turned its attention. It is likely to be a continuing issue, for even if present questions are resolved, the unforeseen character of future scientific progress makes continuing vigilance essential. It must thus be taken into account in any consideration of an international science policy, or of the role of the United Nations family in furthering science and technology.

Arising from this brief survey of some of the principal areas in which science and technology on the one hand and the United Nations system on the other do, or should, interact, it would appear that an examination of the role of the United Nations family in relation to the subject of this symposium — Coordination in the Field of Science and Technology — cannot effectively be approached only in terms of the simple question 'What can the United Nations family do to further science and technology through international cooperation'? While it is an important responsibility of the system to help ensure, through international cooperation, the healthy and socially useful growth of science and technology, they cannot be considered — at the national or international levels — as isolated, independent activities. Science and technology in the developed world pervade all aspects of contemporary society and have become principal sources of innovation and dynamism. In the developing world, technology provides hope for overcoming poverty and underdevelopment. The objectives of science policy at the international level must therefore be similar to the objectives at the national level. In addition to ensuring the growth of science itself, it must make provision for its integration throughout the whole system. It must contribute to the removal of the artificial distinction between developed and developing countries and establish priorities which will help ensure a decent level of existence for all mankind.

If we accept this wider concept of the role of the United Nations family in relation to science and technology and international cooperation, the range of activities to be undertaken must embrace the various needs already mentioned.

While the role of science and technology was not explicitly defined in the earlier concern of the United Nations with economic development for the poorer countries, it was implicit in many of the activities arising within the context of technical assistance. Since the establishment of the United Nations, the role of science and technology in the development process in general has been sharply defined and the place of science policy in national planning has been clarified. As a result, the need for building up science infrastructures in developing countries has received emphasis and the place of science and technology has been recognized in the strategy for the Second United Nations Development Decade. The action program of the General Assembly for the Second United Nations Development Decade states that 'concerted efforts will be made by the developing countries, with appropriate assistance from the rest of the world community, to expand their capability to apply science and technology for development so as to enable the technological gap to be significantly reduced'.[12] This program establishes a target for scientific effort to be attained by developing countries by the end of the decade. No specific targets for developed countries in this respect have been accepted. The Economic and Social Council Committee on Science and Technology for Development has recently recommended, however, that the strategy should be revised to establish targets for the direct support of science and technology programs of developing countries as part of the aid programs of developed countries and for the amount of research undertaken by developed countries on problems of developing countries.[13] It also recommended that goals for science and technology in developing countries should be more sharply defined in relation to development. The passage from the strategy quoted above would be re-drafted to refer to the expansion of the capability of developing countries to 'apply selectively, as well as to develop, science and technology in a manner capable of generating a self-sustaining process of development...'. The adoption of these proposals would emphasize the role of the United Nations family — as well as that of other intergovernmental organizations and of developed countries — in relation to science and technology.

Any consideration of the role of the United Nations family, however, as well as giving highest priority to the urgent needs of developing countries, must be concerned with the interactions of science and technology and mankind as a whole. Some of these effects have been discussed earlier. The impact of science and technology on the political interests of nations — atomic energy, space, the sea-bed, resources — emphasizes the need for the United Nations family to respond at the political level to such challenges as well as to problems arising from the possible effects of science and technology on human rights, or the power of science and technology to shape the pattern of the future. Science and technology themselves need more and more support and policy guidance at the international level because of their increasing cost and complexity and because of the unique opportunities they provide for peaceful and useful international collaboration. But the role of the United Nations family in furthering science and technology through international cooperation must be construed in the context of the roles of science and technology themselves — not as discrete and isolated activities, but as integral parts of the whole fabric of human endeavor.

That the United Nations family should stand in a unique position to further science and technology through international cooperation needs little elaboration. When one considers the system as a whole, its membership of Governments is — to all intents and purposes — universal, thus providing a unique forum for communication. While it is a matter of pride to the scientific community that it has always been international in nature, the integration at the national level of scientific activity with government has made such an international structure necessary for effective coordination. Furthermore, the experience gained since the Second World War by the United Nations system in stimulating and supporting international collaboration far surpasses that of any other international group.

It is obvious, of course, that the role to be played by the United Nations system must be limited by the limitations of the system itself. Thus, while it is tempting for the scientific community to dream dreams and prepare blueprints for a utopian scientific estate, it must be borne in mind that the United Nations system comprises sovereign

Governments and that the system's speed and effectiveness are dependent on the decisions of Member Governments themselves. Nor will it have at its command more financial resources than what governments agree to provide. The political and physical problems involved in consultation make the system slow to respond. Furthermore, as is implicit in a paper by Buzzati-Traverso, the sheer complexity of the organizational system which has grown up largely on a pragmatic basis to meet demands as they have arisen now threatens to be an inhibiting factor to its effectiveness. As pointed out by Sollie, there are many difficult problems to be faced in any undertaking of international coordination.

An examination of the development of science and technology since the Second World War reveals the role already played by the United Nations family in furthering science and technology through international cooperation. It has been the purpose of this paper to draw attention to the fact that the need for such cooperation is greater and more urgent than ever before, but that science and technology can no longer be regarded as activities apart from the mainstream of human existence. If this is accepted, the role of the United Nations family in furthering science and technology through international cooperation must be seen as one of its most important purposes.

What are some of the steps it can take in this respect? The United Nations family must take the lead in encouraging the evolution of an international science policy which would encourage international cooperation in stimulating the vigorous development in science and technology and promote effective application to help ensure the harmonious development of all mankind. In the United Nations family itself, no such comprehensive science policy yet exists. In a recent report,[11] Ritchie-Calder pointed out that in spite of the substantial achievements of the various members of the United Nations family within their fields of competence, the situation is not reassuring. The scope of the scientific activities of the specialized agencies does not encompass the whole range of new developments, nor are those activities always coherent. Interdisciplinary issues tend to be underplayed or bypassed. Member States have not given to the United Nations or the agencies the power of initiative or means commensurate with the new challenges and opportunities within their spheres of activity. The report concluded that with respect to science and technology, the United Nations as presently organized is inadequate to deal with the range and dimensions of the complex tasks involved.

The central machinery in the United Nations for considering science and technology has been a subject of much debate in the Economic and Social Council over the past few years. Since 1964, the Advisory Committee on the Application of Science and Technology to Development, a committee of twenty-four experts sitting in their personal capacities, has advised the Council on the application of science and technology in developing countries and on the coordination of agency scientific programs. The need has been foreseen for some time, however, for a *governmental* committee capable of dealing at the Economic and Social Council level with science and technology problems and responding to ACAST's recommendations. It was pressed by some countries in the debate that such a governmental committee should look at the over-all situation arising from the interaction of science and technology and the United Nations system and report to the General Assembly. The view of the developing countries prevailed, however, and the Committee on Science and Technology for Development, consisting of 54 Governments, is a committee on science and technology for development, albeit the development of *all* mankind. This committee, through which ACAST now reports to the Economic and Social Council, has so far held one session, which was devoted more to political arguments than to the examination of substantive issues concerned with science and technology. While the formation of the Committee on Science and Technology for Development has been a step in the right direction, therefore, it is too early to say whether it will be effective in a decisive way in meeting the need for a global approach to a policy for science and technology.

Until such a policy is established and accepted, the role of the United Nations family in furthering science and technology can only be piecemeal, as it has been in the past. Individual agencies or, at a more detailed level, committees or officials, can facilitate international cooperation and coordination in particular fields. Aid can be given to developing countries, research supported, educational and training programs established, institutions built up, and technology transferred. Cooperative international research projects can be sponsored, studies can be undertaken on the likely effects of new technologies, and governmental machinery set up to deal with political problems arising from science and technology, but if science and technology are to be effectively advanced through international cooperation, the goals of such cooperation must be defined clearly and in some detail. There is a need now for the United Nations system to adapt its organizational structure and work towards the establishment of an over-all policy so that it can provide a more flexible and rapid response to the opportunities and challenges arising from the impact of science and technology at the international and global levels. In this way, science and technology themselves will ultimately be advanced and will play a major role in achieving, in the words of the United Nations Charter, 'international cooperation in solving international problems of an economic, social, cultural and humanitarian character...'. Earth can then become a happier and safer spaceship.

NOTES

1 See for example M. Strong, One Year After Stockholm — An Ecological Approach to Management. *Foreign Affairs,* Vol. 51, No. 4, July 1973.
2 *Science and Technology for Development — Proposals for the Second United Nations Development Decade* (United Nations Publication Sales No. E.70.I.23) p. 23.
3 *Science, Growth and Society — A New Perspective.* OECD, Paris 1971.
4 *Science and Technology for Development* — Report of the United Nations Conference on the Application of Science and Technology for the Benefit of the Less Developed Areas, Vol. VIII, United Nations Publication Sales No. 63:I:28, New York 1963.
5 *World Plan of Action for the Application of Science and Technology to Development.* United Nations Publication Sales No. E.71.II.A.18, New York 1971.
6 *International Development Strategy: Action Programme of the General Assembly for the Second United Nations Development Decade.* United Nations Publication Sales No. E.71.II.A.2) paragraphs 60 to 64.
7 Caryl P. Haskins, Science and Policy for a New Decade. *Foreign Affairs,* Vol. 49, No. 2, Jan. 1971.
8 UN Economic and Social Affairs Council, Committee on Science and Technology for Development: Science and Technology in the Second United Nations development Decade International Development Strategy — Note by the Secretary-General. E/C.8/10, 31 January 1973.
9 Eugene B. Skolnikoff, *The International Imperatives of Technology — Technological Development and the International Political System.* Institute of International Studies, University of California Research Series No. 16, 1972.
10 Christopher Freeman, Malthus with a Computer, in *Thinking About the Future — A Critique of the Limits to Growth,* Chatto and Windus for Sussex University Press, 1973.
11 Lord Ritchie-Calder: *New Dimensions and Opportunities in the Application of Science and Technology to Development and the Role of the United Nations Family.* United Nations Economic and Social Council. E/5238/Add.1, 26 January 1973.
12 *International Development Strategy — Action Programme of the General Assembly for the Second United Nations Development Decade* (United Nations Publication Sales No: E.71.IIA.2).
13 United Nations, Official Records of the Economic and Social Council, Fifty-fifth Session, Supplement No. 4 (E/5272): Committee on Science and Technology for Development — Report of the First Session.

SCIENCE FOR DEVELOPMENT

Adriano Buzzati-Traverso, Rome

Early on in the First Development Decade (1960–1970), the United Nations organized the Conference on the Application of Science and Technology for the Benefit of the Less Developed Areas (Geneva, 1963). The 'revolution of raising expectations', which was occurring in the Less Developed Countries (LDC), seemed to have identified in science and technology the panacea that was going to solve the problems of poverty, disease, and backwardness, in a short time.

On the basis of the recommendations of the governmental conference, the United Nations established the high-level Advisory Committee on the Applications of Science and Technology and the Office of Science and Technology at their headquarters. In the following years the United Nations themselves, the specialized Agencies, regional intergovernmental organizations, and Governments created a myriad of bodies, committees, councils, working groups, etc., and the world was flooded by a deluge of good intentions and printed paper.

Ten years later the situation was best synthesized by Raoul Prébish: the Development Decade was the 'Decade of Frustration'. Some have even come to believe that the so-called applications of science and technology have worked against the efforts of development of the Third World. Thus Théo Lefèvre, Minister for scientific research of Belgium, wrote recently: 'Force nous est de constater que, sous l'effet de la science, l'écart ne fait qu'augmenter entre les pays industrialisés et ceux du tiers monde'. Something has gone wrong, but there is hardly unanimity on the diagnosis of what has gone wrong. The situation of the organization of science and technology in the developing countries, can be summarized in Steven Dedijer's words: 'under-developed science in under-developed countries'.

Innumerable books and articles have been published, and an untold series of meetings has been organized throughout the world, to analyze the problem, express faith in the thaumaturgic virtues of modern science and technology, and recommend to Governments and private bodies the investment of larger shares of their revenues for a much more intensive and widespread use of science and technology to overcome the pressing problems of the Developing Countries. The Governments of the latter have been urged to set up special bodies for the developments of science policy at the national level, and such an appeal was met by a remarkable response. In spite of much enthusiasm, the economic and social conditions of the developing countries have, with few exceptions, been worsening, when compared with those of North America, the USSR, Europe, and Japan: the wealthy are becoming wealthier and the poor poorer; and the same trend seems to prevail within each separate country. Exceptions might be countries with great self-reliant capabilities (People's Republic of China) or massive doses of American investment (South Korea).

Of course, the phrase 'the developing world' is no more than a convenient shorthand symbol, embracing countries as diverse ethnically, culturally, and in every way, as mankind itself. These diversities extend to economic development: to levels of past achievement, to rates of present growth, to future prospects.

Measures designed to aid the developing world as a whole thus face the problem of being effective for, and relevant to, Brazil and Bhutan, Singapore and Somalia, Turkey and Tanzania. In particular, many development specialists argue that the very poorest countries, being without the bases of economic development, lack the capacity to absorb the sophisticated assistance essential for the more rapidly developing countries.

How can science and technology be applied to improve the conditions of people whose styles of life are fundamentally different from those of the countries where scientific and engineering research have been developed? Criteria followed by governments and industries in the advanced countries simply cannot be applied in vast regions of the world. Indeed the book *The Careless Technology* offers a variety of examples of major mistakes incurred with the best of intentions. On the basis of the analysis of past failures and of the complexity of the problems at hand, novel policies are just beginning to be outlined. For example, the Report of the Eighth Session of the U.N. Committee for Development Planning (1972) appears as an important and radical document. It contains a number of ideas that are both fundamental to the concept of development planning, and to the use of science and technology for that purpose. The following list of 21 points is intended as a quick digest: they are arranged under the headings of Policy, Economics, Technology, Agriculture, Environment, and Conclusion.

Policy
(1) 'In some developing countries (the implication is in many) the distribution of income and wealth has become even more unequal in recent years'.

57

(2) Problems of mass poverty are 'massive, growing, and urgent' and mostly require radical action, with poverty elimination moved from the periphery to the centre of development planning.

(3) This calls, in some cases, for 'substantial modifications to present approaches to planning; in others, radically new approaches'. The implication is that there is little hope for present polcies: 'conventional policies are seldom sufficient'.

(4) It is more important to eliminate extreme poverty than it is to reach a given target for economic growth or domestic saving.

(5) Developing countries should support policies for development which use methods and institutions different from their own.

Economics

(6) Developing countries may be forced to choose between economic growth and the elimination of poverty. The Committee minces its words, but obliquely favours the latter policy.

(7) Industrial development should be assessed by the real benefits it produces and not by its profitability; the former should be encouraged by a system of shadow pricing.

(8) The industrial economies should be restructured to facilitate imports from developing countries.

(9) An orientation of small-scale, labour-intensive industrial products such as clothes, shoes, textiles, and domestic utensils would follow from a more egalitarian income distribution.

(10) '. . . good planning cannot proceed without an appreciation of the social costs and benefits of projects at the micro-economic level'.

Technology

(11) A contributing factor to the increasing gap between rich and poor in developing countries 'has been the labour-saving bias of certain kinds of technological change associated with development'.

(12) Encouragement should be given to small or medium-scale industries making light equipment using labour-intensive methods and local resources. Such industries are more efficient than the mass production of gadgets.

(13) Science and technology should be used to produce economic growth by discovering labour-intensive techniques which reduce unemployment and save capital.

(14) Strong and perceptive international assistance should be given for the development of alternative technologies.

Agriculture

(15) 'The objective of a prosperous rural sector needs to be at the centre of the strategy against mass poverty'.

(16) Small-scale agriculture should be given particular interest because 'output per acre is usually higher on small holdings than on large farms'. It is even recommended that very small plots be given to families to feed themselves.

(17) Agricultural products should be diversified (rather than increasingly specialized).

(18) The policy of agricultural mechanization should be re-examined wherever it affects unemployment.

Environment

(19) Development and environmental concerns are not competing but are complementary and mutually supporting.

(20) Lack of development is itself a reflection of a poor nutritional and sanitary environment.

Conclusion

(21) 'It is in the common interest of mankind in the coming decades to formulate global development strategies and take more and more efficient measures for their implementation, in order to achieve a more balanced social and economic development throughout the world and a more harmonious relationship between man and nature.'

Such a document seems to indicate that we are approaching a turning point in the philosophy of aid for development, both in economic terms and in the uses of scientific and technological research.

From the point of view of the economist, the new approach has been recently well expressed by Samir Amin, director of the African Institute for Economic Development and Planning, in an article with the significant title 'Growth is not development'. He writes:

'The Euro-American school of economists', would have us believe that the prosperity of the world depends on the extension of Western institutions to the developing countries which find themselves on the periphery of the capitalist system. They overlook the fact that the evolution of human societies does not progress in orderly fashion through the extension of institutions from one nation to another or across cultural frontiers. It takes place in spurts of creative energy when a formerly dependent society breaks the bonds that fettered it. The centre has the power, but the future lies with the periphery. This is not the kind of view which the master civilizations like to hear, and when it is voiced, they tend to ignore it. More than a century ago, Alexis de Tocqueville warned that power was shifting away from Europe to America and Russia, but it took the bankers of Queen Victoria, of the Third French Republic and of William I of Germany another 50 years to find out how right he had been.'

The same blindness affects those Euro-American centred economists whose education seems to have stopped with the absorption of the Anglo-Saxon metaphysic which sees the universe as peopled by 'economic men', all equal in their aspirations, all subject to the same immutable laws of economic behaviour, all obediently and happily fulfilling their preordained functions and acting alternately as 'producers' and 'consumers'. It is a remarkably convenient abstraction which permits the 'analyst' to dispense with any notions of culture, nationality, social class, or with the power struggle between those that rule and those that are in a position of dependence. It reduces political and economic analysis to the use of a few simple tools, accessible to anyone who can read compound interest tables and knows how to manipulate a slide-rule. A few statistical formulations — particularly gross domestic product, broken down per head of population — become the ultimate measure of things, the key to the mystery of historical processes. Never mind that it is a measure developed for use in industrial societies and that it makes no sense in the developing, largely rural, often subsistence economies of the Third World; it is an easy statistic to throw around and it avoids the necessity of any further thought and reflection.

The high-priest of this cult, and the man who most perfectly expressed the mechanistic and linear approach to development, is of course Walt W. Rostow with his so-called 'theory' of the stages of economic growth.

The Rostowian metaphysic has given rise to an enormous amount of activity in the Euro-American school of economics, in which an endless succession of projections try to establish the future growth rates of far-off lands. Huge wall-maps are marked up in different colours and shadings to distinguish between those countries that will reach the 'take-off' point in the year 2000, those which will make it by 2050, and those unfortunates who will get there still later. As a means of predicting likely realities of the future the whole thing makes of course no sense at all Experienced fiction writers could do better.

How could such a gigantic aberration take place? It is basically an unwitting hoax that was perpetrated through a simple piece of sleight-of-hand when the term 'economic growth' was first likened to, and then gradually substituted for, the term 'development'. Today, as the most casual glance at any relevant literature will show, the two are used interchangeably to designate the same thing. Yet they are concepts, which, although related, deal with profoundly different matters. Growth is essentially a measure of a few relatively easily identifiable units of output; development is an historical process which encompasses not only production, but the entire economic and social life of a nation in transition; its health, education, social outlook, the dynamism of its political institutions, in fact the total life of the nation . . .

An aura of mystery surrounds the multinational corporation and it is important that we understand its workings.

One of the claims made by the multinationals is that such corporations transfer technology. They do not. They sell technology and they sell it under highly monopolistic conditions. In a world where everything is bought and sold, technology is a merchandise like any other, although perhaps an unusually complex one. Its constituent parts are machinery and equipment, skilled labour which knows how to use them, knowledge of processes and markets, raw materials and other inputs. The market for technology is a highly controlled one, which gives the multinationals a large element of monopoly in their field. They use it to draw the maximum possible profit from their dealing with the peripheral countries.

The amount spent by the developing world on the acquisition of technology is already considerable — estimated at $1.5 billion a year and rising annually by some 20 per cent. Moreover, the product they buy is by no means always adapted to the conditions under which it will be used. The highly centralized research and development of the multinational companies is not primarily directed at the conditions obtaining on the periphery. When it comes to developing countries, the right questions are not asked. Among them is the important one on how the new technology will affect the broad mass of the people.

The inadequacy of the technology bought makes itself felt in different ways. Growing unemployment is in many cases associated with new technical processes. Moreover, it is by no means the highest kind of technology that is 'transferred'. The multinationals follow the well-known pattern under which the industries which need low-paid labour are sent abroad while the highly skilled, high return industries — software, electronics, space, atomic and solar energy, to name a few — are kept at home. The experience of countries like Taiwan, Hong Kong, and Singapore, which have received 'runaway industries', shows that the multinational corporations merely serve to deepen the inequalities in the already existing international division of labour.

The answer clearly is that the developing countries must create their own research and development, not to imitate, but to assimilate and invent the processes that are suitable to their needs. Such an initiative will undoubtedly run into the opposition of the multinationals.

The arrogant nationalism of the rich should cause us concern; it blinds too many people to the real problems of the Third World. The much-touted integration of the Third World into the world market is doomed to fail through an inherent contradiction. On the one hand it stirs up the desire of the people of the periphery for real development; on the other hand it effectively closes the doors to the growth of national free enterprise systems set up to meet the economic and social needs of the population, and which, historically, are the forerunner of a genuine, universal post-capitalist and socialist society.

As long as this contradiction remains, the countries of the periphery must either create their own ground-breaking forms of social organization or they must perish. This is merely another way of saying that the law of progress through clash of cultures is as valid today as it has ever been. And there can be no doubt that in mankind's search for new creative interrelationships the Third World has much to contribute, if only because its contribution is such an overall precondition of its survival. The rich world has much to lose if it ignores this contribution of the poor and merely goes on congratulating itself on the progress of a civilization which aims at nothing more than a constantly growing consumption of gadgets by an alienated and dependent élite.

'Aid' is still largely viewed as a palliative designed to give narrow support to the continuation of an unequal international division of labour. One could conceive of a genuine international transfer of resources of the rich to the poor once it is universally accepted that the existing division of labour can be scrapped and a more equitable one take its place. The United Nations could play a role, even a modest one, in bringing about such a change. To do so, the U.N. would have to become more than a channel of transmission of established ideologies and assume the role of spokesman for the countries of the periphery.'

From the point of view of the scientist, it is worth quoting Dr C. M. Varsavsky, an Argentinian physicist:

> The subject of aid to science and technology in developing countries is extremely complicated and deserves further study. Although many agencies have proposed, and even implemented, various policies, it is not at all clear that such policies are the best; they are in fact considered by many to be detrimental to the nations receiving the aid . . .
>
> Many of the aid programs to scientists in underdeveloped countries are, in my opinion, aberrations that develop from the mistake of confusing Science with the Practice of Science. Many well-intentioned planners believe that since Science is universal, the same type of science can, and should, be practised everywhere. Few realize that although the law of gravity may be universal, it is very different for an American or a Russian physicist to work on gravity waves than it is for a Bolivian or Angolian one. And what makes it different is not just the immediate surroundings of the scientist (libraries, laboratories, and assistants) but — far more fundamental — it is the differences in cultural, social and economic background of the scientists as citizens of the different countries. The efforts to impose 'developed' science in underdeveloped countries end up, in most cases, with the alienation of the scientist from the rest of the country. He begins to feel more at home in a foreign university than in his own, and frustrated because he has much greater difficulties in carrying out his research than his colleagues in developed countries. Such alienation makes him more dedicated to his research than to his country, and soon leads to emigration. The proposed International Science Foundation, or the Trieste Centre, purport to 'keep him at home' by giving him a lick of the developed ice-cream. This is nonsense. The way to keep him at home is to make him feel part of the home and a contributor to the betterment of the home. This can only be achieved if a native science is developed, that responds to the needs, to the socio-economic structure, and to the cultural background of the country.
>
> The view just presented differs strongly, of course, from that shared by most scientists in the developed countries and by the 'universalist' scientists of the underdeveloped ones. But there are many who, like myself, do not think that the 'number of publications in foreign journals' should be the measuring rod for 'scientific goodness' in underdeveloped countries.
>
> Time has come for a reappraisal of the objectives of man. We

have the experience of several thousands of years of civilization, a phenomenal technology, and the scientific method. With such tools, and a staff of both social and exact scientists, we should be able in a Happiness Research Institute to formulate objectives — and ways of reaching them — to make humanity happier.'

According to points of view of the type quoted, the major mistake made thus far is derived from the unwarranted assumption that there exists only one path to economic and social development of a country, that which was followed by Europe and North America. In view of the great difference in their physical conditions and resources, in their cultural and traditional background, and in their local interests, the developing countries should adopt original and probably unprecedented patterns of development. For such a purpose there is a need for building up an indigenous scientific and technological potential aimed at contributing directly to the self-realization of each country or region, consistent with the aspiration of the people.

A thorough assessment should be carried out of what the LDCs can realistically expect from science and technology; the study should be made not by the usual committee of experts, but by teams of scientists, engineers, economists, and sociologists which should essentially belong to or be able to spend extensive periods in the countries or regions concerned, so as to reach a concrete 'feeling' of the needs. Imagination and inventiveness will be required. Probably, in the years to come, a new discipline will emerge: *science for development,* that would include those aspects of natural and allied social sciences that relate to the problems of LDCs. Such a broad definition includes both basic and applied topics. The problem of launching a new, multidisciplinary area of research is not new to the recent history of international science: a quarter of a century ago, molecular biology, oceanography, and space science were at the stage in which science for development is today.

The task ahead is that of bringing to the attention of the international scientific community, and particularly of the scientists of the industrialized countries, the existence of exciting and important problems, to make available research money, to publicize that availability and to provide the communications necessary for the establishment of a cohesive new discipline: science for development. There exists in the world an immense reservoir of talented scientists and engineers who are anxious to demonstrate to the world and to themselves that their efforts are important and useful. The mobilization of this largely untapped resource is likely to become the chief instrument for achieving a balanced human and economic development of countries of the Third World, through the realization of their human potentialities and increased productivity from their available natural resources.

Such a novel approach would also require substantial changes at the level of international institutions involved in the application of science and technology to development. In 1968 the Advisory Committee on the Applications of Science and Technology to Development (ACAST) called the attention of the U.N. to the need for streamlining methods, procedures, and structures. Since then the situation has deteriorated further, through the establishment of an even larger number of bodies, committees, groups, panels, etc. At present the number of these bodies under direct U.N. responsibility, including the Regional Economic Commissions but excluding the U.N. Specialized Agencies, exceeds 100! The cause of this excessive growth lies in the fact that new committees and working groups have been added to those already active to comply with new resolutions passed in a number of different U.N. bodies. These new bodies are often created without regard for the responsibilities and functions of previously existing ones, and compound the problem of bureaucratic proliferation.

As the most recent example of such a state of affairs, we can refer to the high-level governmental committee created two years ago by the Economic and Social Council of the United Nations, in which 54 countries participate, called the Committee on Science and Technology for Development (CSTD). The new body was established to plan and coordinate United Nations' policies for bringing science and technology to bear on the problems of developing countries. It was created with the hope that it would provide a strong and effective voice in the development of UN science policies. Unfortunately, as reported in the scientific journal *Nature*: '... that hope dimmed a little last month when the committee's first meeting got bogged down in a political dispute, failed to tackle most of the items on its agenda and ended in uproar'.

The state of confusion now reached and the novel approach to the problem call for prompt measures to make the UN system more effective in this area, and also to coordinate its actions with those of other organizations with similar aims. Such measures cannot be identified or implemented unless a thorough study is made of the present situation. It would consist of the following parts:

(1) *Survey of UN and other bodies active in the promotion of science and technology in LDCs*

This part would consist of a detailed survey of the existing agencies, bodies, committees, panels, groups, etc. active in the area. The survey would include the whole UN system, inter-governmental agencies not belonging to the UN system, national agencies of wealthier countries, private foundations, and multinational corporations operating for the benefit of LDCs. The survey would include data on terms of reference, data of establishment, reasons why the body was created, relationships to other bodies, etc.

(2) *Quantitative analysis of (1) in terms of financial investments and results*

This part would present data on the costs of operation of the various bodies identified under (1) and will attempt to evaluate the concrete actions that have resulted from the activities of the said bodies.

(3) *Critical analysis of the present situation*

On the basis of data presented under (1) and (2), a critical analysis would be carried out of the efficiency of current operations, attempting to identify the major pitfalls.

This part of the study should candidly appraise not only present inefficiencies in terms of proliferation of structures, but should also extend the evaluation to methods of operation of various bodies, relationships among them, organization of conferences, production of reports, ratios between staff on long-range contracts and short-range consultants, criteria for selection of consultants and experts, duplication and repetition of efforts, relations between work and time in headquarters and in the field, amounts of paper used per structural and time unit, costs of translations, etc.

For this purpose studies in loco should be made not only at the seats of the various agencies, in consultation with their executive heads, but also in a representative sample of some twenty LDCs, in order to determine real levels of achievement as compared with original expectations, and also to identify difficulties in the national machineries devoted to the request, acceptance, and utilization of foreign aid.

The study and the launching of the new discipline — science for development — are admittedly ambitious tasks. But the world's intellectual potential, financial means, and good-will must be mobilized to catalyse the development of the people according to their aspirations, without well-meaning impositions on the part of the powerful.

NEW DIRECTIONS IN DEVELOPMENT

Glenn T. Seaborg, University of California

We traditionally have held that objectivity is a fundamental aspect of science and scientific research. But perhaps nowhere is it more difficult to be objective these days than in analyzing the roles of science and technology in international development. In fact, the entire matter of development is one filled with strong subjective beliefs, with varying opinions on what goals should be set and the best means of achieving them.

Discussing development is a difficult matter for a number of reasons. First of all, in considering development we are dealing fundamentally with issues that determine human well-being or human deprivation, human happiness or human misery, and perhaps in the long run human survival altogether.

At the same time as we are gripped by these large issues, we are also torn between feelings of international altruism and a degree of ingrained national self-interest. We still live and work on these two levels.

In addition, as scientists, specialists, and members of various organizations, we hold, and tend to remain loyal to, certain points of view which are bound to influence our outlook on the total picture, large and complex and multidimensional as it is. We may be Neo-Malthusians, advocates of economic adjustments, believers in the 'technological fix', or champions of a regulatory approach.

But also, most of us have lived and worked in the so-called 'real world' long enough to be its captives intellectually and emotionally. That is, we are realists; we know the forces of politics, of economics, of human habit, of all the factors that inhibit necessary change or exact their toll when rapid change is thrust upon the world either through new ideas or new technologies.

As a result of all this, a certain pattern seems to take shape whenever men of science gather in international meetings to discuss the role of science and technology in development. One can usually sense an extended fervor in the air because of the very nature of the subject and its implications for mankind. We know what is at stake. We know the potential power of science and technology for good. We have seen it work in the past. We see it at work today. And we want to see it work in the future. But our background, our interests, our 'realism' tend to shade our vision and our ability to shape the alternatives that must take root in the world today. We resort to a considerable degree of linear thinking, to looking at and extrapolating from historical trends and examples, and to projecting futures based on extensions of some, rather than building the kind of new world that the projections might indicate is necessary.

But there is hope. In recent years some of our projections, particularly those involving resources and environmental problems, have shocked us into newer modes of thinking, and these are beginning to affect our ideas about development. One can hear rumblings of these effects. They followed the publication of the study *The Limits to Growth,* supported by the Club of Rome. They surfaced at the Stockholm conference and in the planning of the UN Environmental Program, in terms of possible conflicts between the needs of development and the protection of the environment. We are bound to hear more on this score as efforts are made to internalize the cost of a healthy environment in the world's industries. We also are going to hear more on matters of population and population distribution, land development and tenure, food, resources, trade, aid, the seas and space — to name a few of the topics that will provoke new thinking in the light of development needs and trends.

In my brief remarks here I would like to construct a type of framework that might be conducive to some of that newer thinking, and within that framework offer some suggestions as to ways that science and technology might serve development more rationally and constructively.

Let me begin by referring to a concept of global development upon which I speculated a few years ago in speaking to an international conference on 'Environment and Society in Transition'.[1] In my remarks at that time I expressed the philosophical belief that we — the human race — were evolving from a condition of tribal man to a truly organic mankind, a global civilization that would eventually live in harmony with itself and its environment. I stressed the point that a global civilization could exist but momentarily on this earth if it were to act as a parasite or cancer, that it had to establish a nonexploitive, closed-cycle way of life, and that this could only be done by the formulation and application of a new scientific outlook and new ecological-technological relationship.

In the intervening years all that I have seen and heard in the world has reinforced my belief in this idea. And it is particularly applicable to the matter of development and the relationships between the developing and developed nations. Development must take the form of a globally integrated process in which the natural and human resources of each nation become part of a system through which each will benefit and fulfill its potential in a way that allows the entire system to thrive. Hence, an organic mankind — a system of nations — will be much the same as a healthy individual who enjoys good health because all his organs and parts are functioning in a balanced way, contributing to each other and to the whole man.

This biological analogy can be alluded to in many ways relating to our world civilization. One way, of course, is to think in terms of a global metabolism into which industrial production must be worked so as to assure that the flow of materials and energy in and out of manmade systems does not interfere with the cycles of natural systems. The environmental movement has made us fully aware of this requirement and the kind of activity that must take place to meet it.

Another way is to think of emerging mankinds as one might conceive of an unborn individual, perhaps in the stage of an early fetus. At this point the brain and the nervous system precede the development of the organs and skeletal structure of the body. One could liken this to the global situation in which our lines of communication first reach out to the various parts of the world and their peoples. This is followed by early international economic activity and trade which act as a growing circulatory system helping to feed and build the individual organs. Pursuing the analogy still further, we might compare technological growth to increased hormonal activity, and economic growth through industrialization to muscular and metabolic activities.

Of course these analogies are far from perfect. But I think they can help to illustrate, if only in a crude way, something which is occurring in the world of which we must be aware — namely, that the formation of a global system bearing some resemblance to an organic one has been taking place.

But there are now indications that its development is entering a new phase where the system must regulate itself so that its parts mature in a way best suited to their own health and that of the system. In realistic terms, nations cannot and should not all grow in the same way, attempting to become copies of other nations in different regions with different resources, backgrounds, cultures, and needs. Each must develop in a manner, at a pace, and toward goals best suited to the needs of its own people while contributing to the overall needs of the world.

How is all this to come about? Do we have in our global system the equivalent of a DNA or RNA code destined to regulate our growth?

I believe that, broadly speaking, it may exist in science, and that a major role — if not *the* major role — of science in the coming years is going to be the direction that scientific thinking can give to development. This direction should take place in many forms and on many levels.

At the highest level it should determine and recommend a system of integrated development based on economic readjustments — combining trade, aid, monetary measures — designed to balance better the growth of developing and advanced nations. Part of this balance would probably be achieved by setting up conditions that would favor the production and export of goods from countries best suited to produce them, in terms of resources, environment, labor, and other conditions. Developing nations badly need this kind of production and trade advantage. As a recent report by the U.S. Secretary of State indicates: 'Trade is more important than aid for developing countries. Export earnings account for nearly four-fifths of their total foreign exchange resources.'[2]

Economics must be used as a basic and applied science to accomplish this end, just as it is being used as a means of instituting environmental changes. And as economic forces do not operate in a vacuum, the social and political sciences must be used in conjunction with them. Of course this implies that we foster an international commitment that somehow supersedes many of today's national interests and nationalistic feelings. Ironically, these seem to be on the rise today at a time that begs for closer international cooperation. Perhaps, therefore, the entire key to the future rests on whether the nations of the world — and particularly their leaders — can be made to see the folly, the shortsightedness and, ultimately, the disaster of a divided world. And this is true not only in terms of rich and poor, or ideological division, but in the matters of advantages of natural and human resources, including scientific and technical knowledge.

(Let me indicate at this point that there are many organizations and individuals in the world who have strongly advocated this point of view, or ones similar to it, for some time. I think their ranks and influence are growing. Foremost among them are, of course, the specialized agencies of the United Nations — particularly the United Nations Development Program (UNDP), which assists projects in over 130 developing countries. The individuals are too numerous to mention but a few that come to mind because of their tireless efforts over the years are Barbara Ward, Aurelio Peccei, and the late Lester Pearson.)

In dealing with this difficult matter of integrated international development I believe that in addition to the new work of established organizations such as the UNDP, we will see important scientific contributions coming from new organizations such as the International Federation of Institutes for Advanced Study, the UN Environmental Program, and the International Institute for Applied Systems Analysis being established in Vienna. The work of such organizations should establish a better scientific basis for the type of development compatible with environmental needs and the technological change taking place in the world.

This leads me to the second level of the role science should play in directing development. If the first was helping plan global integration, the second must be working on regional and national levels to see that each country and each area develops in a way that is best for its own people and environment. This, unfortunately, is bound to be a matter of some controversy over the years. There are several reasons. A basic one lies with the very notion of development as various people conceive it. To many, development has become synonymous with industrialization, particularly with the process of industrialization through which the Western World went in the 19th century. We know today that technologically speaking much of that process can be bypassed, but also that many of the conditions that made it possible in Europe and the United States do not exist in a number of areas that are striving for industrialization today. The kind of industry that most developing nations could sustain today does not have the labor requirement that would absorb the large influx of workers being forced to leave rural areas because of changing agricultural practices. A whole new outlook toward the development process is necessary, and is, in fact, seriously being studied and discussed throughout the world.

In essence this outlook emphasizes the need to stem the influx of population to already crowded urban areas by a combination of two related efforts. One is new rural development — building the need for rural employment based on agriculture-related needs. The other is the development of small-scale industry in outlying areas, existing villages or new towns, calling for less capital-intensive and more labor-intensive production. Much of both of these — the agricultural and industrial work — would involve what is coming to be known as Intermediate (or Appropriate) Technology: relatively light machinery and equipment that allow the productive employment of more people but eliminate the backbreaking labor and drudgery historically associated with labor-intensive production. Intermediate Technology should also be of the type to take advantage of local conditions and resources. It should be able to harness the natural energy most available in the area — solar, wind, water, or geothermal power. It should be designed for simple operation, service, and repair. And it should be low in cost and maintenance. The creation of such technology offers a great challenge to science and engineering today.

The reasons we only recently have begun to emphasize this kind of technology are many. Barbara Ward stated a major one when she wrote several years ago:

> The technology which is dominant in the world today is not always appropriate to the needs of the developing countries — and this for a very simple reason. The whole weight of economic research and of investment in further research is virtually confined to the developed countries and has, for 50 years and more, taken the form of trying to find labor-saving methods of production.[3]

This, of course, is a difficult pattern to change. Viable, profitable markets must be created, literally overnight, if this new kind of technology is to be introduced. And its introduction calls for considerable other social and economic change in a country, even if we assume that the country is willing to recognize the need for it. This in itself poses major problems. Many countries believe they can be successful in following the conventional process of industrialization and that any efforts to convince them otherwise are an infringement on, or an insult to, their national sovereignty. Some are already in the midst — and the agony — of that process, with the result that many have a rate of unemployment and underemployment ranging up to more than 30 percent. No one knows what the outcome of this will be, but it seems likely that much social upheaval and human misery will take place before it becomes clear.

In speaking of this new type of development involving the effort to maintain productive and healthy populations away from the large urban areas, to redevelop rural regions and locate small-scale industry there with the help of intermediate technology, let me emphasize that there are examples of this under way. One example of how a single item of intermediate technology can establish a linkage between agriculture and small-scale industry has been the tubewell. As one development economist has pointed out:

> In the last decade entire towns and sections of towns have grown and developed almost entirely around the domestic manufacture of diesel engines for private tubewells, other tubewell parts, and of course the drilling installation and repair operations. The agricultural investment in private tubewells has encouraged ad-

ditional investment in small-scale manufacturing, very little of which actually gets measured for national account purposes.[4]

Walter Elkan, the economist who wrote that statement, emphasized the importance of establishing in developing countries small-scale industries that have what he calls 'backward and forward linkage' — that is, which stimulate related industries that supply materials and services to the central item being produced, and also create future needs. Such an industry would be building construction, for example, which calls for raw and finished materials and, when completed, stimulates the need for furnishings and household goods which might be manufactured within the country.

In the future we should see, with the help of good international cooperation in science and technology, some productive combinations of intermediate and high technology. One of these might be the use of inexpensive television receivers in remote rural areas, and small villages and towns in developing nations, to make use of the telecasting of educational and technical information from communications satellites. This combination could bring to people — who are otherwise isolated or lack the means — education for their children and themselves, information to aid them in their farming and the marketing of their products, important weather information, and general news and entertainment. India will provide a prime test for education via satellite television when in 1975 the United States makes available to her its Applications Technology Satellite. This satellite, to be positioned in an equatorial orbit, will be available to India for six hours a day for at least one year under a current agreement. India is now preparing to provide direct telecast from the satellite into receivers in 150,000 villages. Much of the success of satellite television of this type will hinge on the ability to produce and distribute very inexpensive but reliable television receivers. The problem is obvious when we realize that the people who need these sets the most may have an average annual income of about $100. Eventually, we may see a system of nuclear-powered, synchronous satellites in use at about 22,000 miles above the Earth which would allow direct telecast to battery-operated television sets anywhere on earth. At that time it would be to our great advantage to have available a television set comparable with the cheap battery-operated transistor radios so common around the world.

Up to this point, I have spoken of science and technology helping to direct international development from two rational approaches: that of planning and controlling the exchange of resources so as to narrow the gap between rich and poor, and that of encouraging a redirection of development within the developing areas to emphasize employment and dispersed growth based on a different style of industrialization. But science and technology must work, as they always have, on the level of dealing directly with individual problem areas in a disciplinary and interdisciplinary manner. And it is to this level that I want to devote the remainder of my remarks, emphasizing some key problems and some new directions in dealing with them.

Foremost among the problems facing man, and particularly the developing nations, are still those associated with food and health. This is true in spite of the fact that we have made enormous strides in these areas during the past decade, thanks to such men as Norman Borlaug, Carlos Chagas, and others participating in this Symposium.

The Green Revolution must be pursued to its fullest potential throughout the world, and the problems that its initial success has highlighted must receive the fullest attention of science and technology. One of the most important of these has to do with man's use and control of water. In many parts of the world, including those where the Green Revolution has been most successful, food production is highly dependent on weather patterns that have been erratic from year to year; accordingly, we find ourselves fluctuating from years of surplus to years of famine. Periods of droughts or floods seem to be the rule rather than the exception in many areas. While we certainly cannot control the world's weather, we must at least develop a better understanding of it — enough to avoid having the fate of a nation hinge on the coming of a monsoon that never materializes. We also need to intensify our understanding and control of the water cycle throughout the world, to know more about underground water and how better to use it, to increase our knowledge and ability in flood control, to further our efforts in water recycling and desalting technology, and to pursue the possibilities of weather modification.

As recently estimated, our global water demands will increase by about 100 billion cubic meters per year just to keep up with the population increase. We therefore will have to make great efforts in the years ahead in water conservation and technologies for tapping new sources for fresh water.[5]

Another problem area associated with food that demands the best efforts of science around the world is the destruction of food by pests. Up to 50 percent of the world's food that is produced is destroyed before it can be consumed by human beings. It is devoured and spoiled by insects and rodents or is attacked by micro-organisms. It has been estimated that in Africa alone the amount of grain lost annually could feed 55 million people. We clearly need better means of pest control and food preservation and storage throughout the world. There is much promising work being conducted to meet these needs. Some examples are the work of the International Rice Research Institute to breed rice varieties resistant to certain pests, a multi-university research program on integrated methods of pest management being coordinated in the United States by the International Center for Biological Control at the University of California, Berkeley, and programs of the UN's Food and Agricultural Organization and the International Atomic Energy Agency. Most recently a new international organization, the Group for Assistance on Storage of Grain in Africa, has been formed to devote itself to the prevention of postharvest crop losses on that continent. Its members are conducting research and trying to improve traditional methods of storage to reduce the huge destruction of food caused by rodents.

The scientific community around the world must continue to increase its investigations of the seas, particularly as they relate to marine resources and food supply. A better knowledge of such phenomena as coastal upwelling and other natural conditions that influence the growth and movement of fish populations may help us to regulate our exploitation of certain species which seem to be declining just at a time when we are turning increasingly to the sea as a greater source of protein. The fact that international competition in fishing has intensified, to the point of open conflict over off-shore territorial limits in some areas, indicates even more strongly the need for a new era of cooperation in our understanding and uses of the sea. Much has been said over the years about 'farming the seas' but we still remain primarily sea hunters, even to the extent of sometimes accusing each other of poaching. Next year we will have a major United Nations Conference on the Law of the Sea which may settle some of the legal questions concerning our expanding use of the sea's resources. But the time is now overdue when we must develop a true science and technology of the sea, emphasizing aquaculture on oceans and inland. This would be of particular benefit to many of the developing nations, some of which depend heavily on fishing as a source of food and revenue. It even has been suggested that international agreements be made that would favor the developing nations as the world's fisheries because the fishing industry is labor-intensive and can keep large numbers of people employed.

Closely related to the food problems of the developing world is the matter of health. It is this matter that always has been a major focus of the world's science community and continues to be, with new problems taking hold as older ones are solved. In my visits around the world to more than 60 countries, I always have been impressed by the dedication of the medical profession and those engaged in health and biological research, particularly in the developing countries where they seem to be working against such overwhelming odds.

Many of the health problems throughout the developing nations will improve slowly as conditions related to poverty — poor nutrition, sanitary conditions, and education — are improved. Great strides have been made in reducing such major scourges as malaria, tuberculosis, yaws, and the major communicable diseases. Credit for much of this success is due to the World Health Organization (WHO), which coordinates an extensive network of medical science activities around the world on a pitifully small budget. As Martin Kaplan, Director of the Office of Science and Technology of WHO, has pointed out, WHO's activities 'are carried out with a total effective working budget that the sanitation services of many large cities in the United States would consider grossly inadequate, some 100 million dollars annually.'[6] Over a period of the last 15 years WHO's research has made a significant contribution to medical science and technology in, among other things, evaluating the effectiveness of various vaccines and serums, in providing insights into malnutrition, in conducting studies on the biology of many insect vectors and their resistance to insecticides, and in developing nearly 300 biological standards and working preparations to provide baseline references for all countries. Dr. Kaplan sees the unfilled priority areas of WHO's work in science and technology to lie in such matters as: the development of a worldwide health information network, an increase in fundamental and applied research in parasitic diseases, a better understanding of the biology of human reproduction, more knowledge of the effects of toxic chemicals (especially at the molecular level), and improved technological aids for diagnostic and survey procedures. Such aids would be invaluable in mass campaigns against communicable diseases, for population studies in genetics, nutrition, and metabolic disorders. Less expensive technological procedures are also necessary for dealing with environmental and sanitation problems.

In outlining these priority areas of research and development, Dr. Kaplan stressed two major requirements for their success; one was increased funds, the other was greater participation of leading scientists and advanced laboratories. It is on this matter of participation that I want to conclude my remarks. And rather than focus on the role of national and international institutions with which you are familiar, I would like to discuss briefly a new organization whose work we hope will increase the participation of scientists in meeting the needs of developing nations. I say 'we' because of my personal involvement in its initial planning and formation together with Roger Revelle, Robert Marshak, Maurice Levy, Sven Brohult, and many others. I shall also describe briefly another proposal I have made for promoting the contributions of scientists and technologists all over the world to international development.

The organization to which I refer is the recently formed International Foundation for Science (IFS) an organization designed to 'support and encourage scientific research in developing countries by seeking out and supporting promising young scientists'. IFS was formed by a consortium of national scientific academies, research councils, and equivalent organizations in developed and developing countries. The consortium consists, at present, of 21 members, almost equally divided between developing and developed nations.

A major purpose of IFS is to fill a large gap that remains between the efforts of national and intergovernmental organizations in assisting the growth of science and technology in the developing countries through 'institution building' and providing training and advice by outside experts, and the need to support research by individuals and small groups in the universities and research institutions of the poor countries. IFS will focus its efforts on the latter, particularly on supporting the work of younger faculty members and their graduate students in the natural and social sciences. The Foundation hopes to ameliorate the plight of young scientists in the developing countries, who now have little opportunity to develop their own potential, by providing small grants that would enable them to undertake specific research projects, which they have proposed themselves, in their home countries. The emphasis of the grants would be on allowing the scientists to maintain the continuity of their research over a period of years, and on providing them with technicians, instruments, and scientific literature.

Among the criteria for the grants would be the relevance of the proposed research to the needs of the country. The Foundation hopes to encourage cooperation among scientists in the poor countries by seeking proposals in the same field from different countries.

The ideas that went into the formation of IFS were tested over the past few years by contacts — through correspondence and personal visits — between members and associates of the Foundation's Interim Board and officers of national scientific bodies in Asia, Africa, and Latin America. These contacts verified the great need for the type of support IFS will offer.

When the Interim Board of IFS met in Stockholm last February, several kinds of research that the Foundation might support were discussed. Representative of these were: comparative studies of soil fungi that seem to be essential to the successful introduction of new tree crops in areas where they had not previously grown; the microbiology of nitrogen fixation for rice, soy beans, and other crops; the chemistry of natural products, including those which may be of pharmaceutical value; geophysical methods of prospecting for and appraising underground water; the biology of reproduction of fresh water and brackish water fish species that are suitable for fish culture; and studies of social and demographic changes related to the introduction of new agricultural technologies.

The importance of research projects such as these to development is obvious. Furthermore, they have several common characteristics that make them desirable for IFS support. They represent relatively inexpensive research that could be undertaken by individuals or small groups in universities and existing research institutions. Their results contain foreseeable applications. There are competent individual scientists in the developing countries eager to do such research. The training of graduate students could be an integral part of this research. And similar projects in other countries could provide opportunities for cooperative work.

The International Foundation for Science has been launched in the firm belief that there is a substantial reservoir of scientific talent in the developing countries that must be supported and encouraged to grow. Each country should have the opportunity to develop its own cadre of competent young scientists who have, in addition to their scientific and technical knowledge, a first-hand understanding of the problems of their country and an ability to make the most of the outside expertise provided for them by the regional and international scientific organizations and through the scientific exchange programs. We look forward now to seeing the ideas behind the IFS take root, to being able to increase its support and the scope of its work.

In devoting some of my remarks to this new organization for supporting research in the developing countries, I have not meant to play down the important role of the major national and international scientific organizations, several of which I have mentioned and all of which deserve mention and praise. They have done and continue to do outstanding work.

But there has been no widespread activity among individual scientists and engineers throughout the world directed toward the solution of practical contemporary problems and the promotion of human welfare on an international scale. It was with the thought of moving toward the mobilization of such action that I proposed[7] at the recent conference 'Science and Man in the Americas' the formation of a true *American* Association for the Advancement of Science to be followed in due course by a worldwide joining together of national associations of science in an International Association for the Advancement of Science (or perhaps an International Association for the Advancement of Science and Technology).

The many Associations for the Advancement of Science in the countries throughout the world are well suited for action directed toward the application of science and technology in the promotion of human welfare. They are in general noncommercial, nonpolitical associations of scientists and engineers and of other people interested in science and engineering. They are nationwide in scope and include all of the natural and social sciences. In each case the membership is in general open to all without restriction as to scientific qualifications and thus can be referred to as the 'Lower House of Science'. Also, typically, each such national association has organized affiliations with many other associations and societies in its country.

Thus these Associations are, in varying degrees, representative of organized science in the countries in which they operate and can act with the great authority inherent in their broad membership. There are at present some 40 associations of this type with a wide variation in their names. I believe the effectiveness of their member scientists in promoting the contributions of international science and technology to the forging of an organic mankind will be greatly enhanced through some worldwide unification of the present individual efforts.

The work for all of us in science and technology has only begun, in terms of what we might — and what we must — accomplish in world development. The forces that our past accomplishments have set in motion must be controlled and given new direction. The knowledge uncovered by our past efforts raises new questions that demand answers. In dealing with development at this stage we face what may be man's greatest task — essentially taking over where natural evolution has left off in determining the destiny of our species, and perhaps that of the entire planet. Man will be called upon for new wisdom and leadership in meeting this awesome challenge. To not rise to this challenge would be not only to fail that portion of mankind seeking to lift itself from deprivation and despair, but to deprive the world of its first — and perhaps only — chance to unite in a global civilization, one in which all can live in dignity and harmony. I believe we will succeed in our efforts to help build that kind of world.

NOTES
1 Glenn T. Seaborg, The positive power of science, *Environment and Society in Transition* (Proceedings of the International Joint Conference of the American

Geographical Society and the American Division of the World Academy of Art and Science, April 27—May 2, 1970), *Annals* of the New York Academy of Sciences, Vol. 184, 1972, pp. 682—687.

2 *U.S. Foreign Policy, 1972: Report of the Secretary of State.* Department of State Publication 8699, General Foreign Policy Series 274. Washington: Superintendent of Documents, April 1973, p. 42.

3 Barbara Ward, The Decade of Development, *Reshaping the World Economy* (John A. Pincus, ed.). Prentice-Hall, Inc., Englewood Cliffs, 1968, p. 27.

4 Walter Elkan, *Introduction to Development Economics.* Penguin Books, Harmonesworth, England, 1973, p. 115.

5 Jose P. Peixoto and M. Ali Kettoni, The control of the water cycle, *Scientific American*, Vol. 228, No. 4, April 1973, p. 46.

6 Martin Kaplan, Science's role in the World Health Organization, *Science*, Vol. 180, No. 4090, 8 June 1973, p. 1028.

7 Glenn T. Seaborg, Science technology and development: a new world outlook, *Science*, Vol. 181, No. 4094, 6 July 1973, pp. 13—19.

COOPERATION IN SCIENCE AND TECHNOLOGY
— THE OECD APPROACH

Alexander King OECD, Paris

At first sight it may appear surprising that an international organization, dominantly economic in its interests, should support important programs in science and education. The fact is that OECD is concerned with these topics in relation to economic growth and social development as important items of national investment which, although of long-term influence, contribute vitality to society and the economy.

It is only recently that the relationship between science and the economy has received serious attention. Formerly, although it was realized that great new industries such as the electrical, chemical, and pharmaceutical industries had grown essentially on the basis of scientific discovery, economists tended to assume that research was called into being and supported essentially as the result of the operation of economic forces. The growth economics school, however, some fifteen years ago postulated a more direct relationship. Denison, for example, calculated that of the growth of the American economy during this century, only some 40 percent could be ascribed to the classical inputs of capital and labour. The other 60 percent, termed by him the residual factor, was due to a complex of elements amongst which science and education appeared particularly important. In fact, this means that research and education contribute to the quality of manpower and to the quality of capital utilization.

OECD is therefore concerned with science in its broad relationship with economy and society rather than with science for its own sake.

The OECD Approach
OECD programs in science and education have thus a somewhat different orientation from those of other international organizations. They seek to elucidate the relationship between science, economy, and society and to see how research can, through technology and by direct application of the scientific method to the complex problems of society, contribute to national prosperity and social well-being. The Organization does not have any ambition to undertake operational work, to manage scientific projects or programs, or to undertake con-

tinuing service activities. It seeks rather to be a catalyst of policy change, to understand problems, to seek out new approaches and trends, to analyze and integrate these, possibly to demonstrate them in the hope that they may contribute elements of innovation which the member countries can assimilate within their own traditions and their own institutional frameworks. The orientation is outwards towards the countries rather than the organization of international activity for its own sake.

As a consequence of this approach, the science programs of the Organization are continually changing. Once a study is completed or an impulse in a particular direction given to the member countries, the activity is brought to an end and new innovative directions chosen. This necessitates a high intellectual mobility, which has been achieved by running the programs partly by permanent staff, partly by short term experts on each specific item, recruited for the purpose. The staff is highly multidisciplinary, including natural scientists, engineers, economists, and behavioural scientists.

At times such activities give rise to the need for continuing work. This may be ensured by creating small satellite units, each financed separately by those countries interested in participating and willing to pay, sometimes by creating and spinning off independent institutions. Present examples of the former are the program for road research (to be described later), a project on intercity transport needs of the future, a centre for educational innovation, and one for educational buildings. Independent institutes created include a series of international applied research programs which were incubated within the Organization, the European Industrial Research Management Association which includes as its members more than 130 of the largest European firms, and the International Institute for the Management of Technology at Milan.

The country examinations
If the policy of contributing elements of innovation to the individual member countries is to succeed, it is necessary for the secretariat of OECD and its main science committee, the Committe for Scientific and Technological Policy, to understand in as great detail as possible the policies, structures, and problems of each member. To meet this, two systems of country examination were instituted for science and education respectively. The science policy reviews consist of a detailed investigation of the policies, structures, manpower and resource distribution for research and development and their coupling with national objectives, particularly economic and social. These are undertaken by firstly preparing a thorough background description

of the national situation, its economy, industrial structure, research, and academic system. This is generally compiled by an OECD staff member or a rapporteur appointed for the purpose. The background report, although it may formulate certain problems, normally avoids all value judgements; it is of course subject to corrections of fact or accuracy of data by the country concerned.

The next stage is a visit of a group of eminent scientific personalities to the country under examination. They are selected after consultation between the secretariat and the national authorities and frequently include an economist. Having studied the background report, they visit the country in question, discussing its policies and problems with ministers, science administrators, representatives of the scientific and academic communities, and industrialists. Their report formulates the main issues as they see them and poses a number of fundamental questions. It is issued entirely as the personal assessment of the examiner and does not represent a formal OECD position. The next stage is the 'confrontation meeting' held either in Paris or in the country under examination, at which a team of the national science policy leaders is cross-questioned at length by the examiners in the presence of science policy representatives of the other member countries, who are able to raise supplementary questions. Finally a report is published which consists of the background report, the examiners' report, and a précis of the confrontation. Initially these examinations were basically descriptive and somewhat superficial, but as confidence in their objectivity was gradually established they became progressively more searching and their constructive criticism is generally welcomed. Countries normally ask for such examinations at a time when their policies and structures for science and technology are being assessed, to provide an objective and constructive view from people with wide experience of such problems elsewhere. In many cases these examinations have had a considerable influence on national policy — mainly, it must be admitted, in the smaller countries. The OECD countries are responsible for nearly three-quarters of the world's research and development. A major proportion of the residuum is undertaken in the Soviet Union. A substantial review was therefore made of the evolution of policies for science in that country, without, of course, the confrontation.

Science policy

A major activity in which OECD has been a pioneer is in its advocacy of the creation within each country of a coherent science policy. Ten years ago the concept was hardly recognized in Europe. During the first months of OECD, however, the Secretary General convened a small group of high-level experts, both natural scientists and economists, which met under the chairmanship of M. Piganiol of France and discussed the concept of science policy and mechanisms for its creation. Their report, 'Science and the Policies of Governments', pointed out that there are two aspects of the problem. Firstly the need to establish policies for the management of science and the allocation of resources for its support between the many alternative claims. Secondly the need to consider the impact of science on other elements of national policy.

A policy for science has become necessary because of a widespread recognition of its importance in many aspects of national life — defence, industrial development, health, agriculture, and even national prestige and foreign affairs. This has encouraged governments to spend money on research which now amounts to a sizeable proportion of national expenditure, becoming an investement which requires care in selection and management such as is given to other investment items. However, since research contributes to development in so many fields, decision as to the allocation of its resources is a complex matter, essentially political, as an element within the general policies for a whole series of activities such as the economy, health, defence, and education.

However, science differs from other sub-systems within the total national system in that a proportion of its resources has to be diverted to its maintenance and continuous self-renewal. This is the function of fundamental research, which not only uncovers new knowledge but produces a community of individuals who are constantly sharpening their perceptions and insights at the frontiers of knowledge. Such research is essentially international in nature, it advances by contribution from all countries, and its results are freely published. Although it can be regarded as a long-term investment, its exploitation may not necessarily take place within the country which supports it but rather in places where its significance for application is perceived and where capital and markets are available. This basic difference in investment characteristics separates science as such from technology.

It has often been argued that since expenditure of men and money on basic research is a contribution to the pool of world knowledge into which all who wish may dip, countries could well minimize their fundamental research efforts and concentrate on application. This proves to be short-sighted and self-defeating, since it is only through training in fundamental research that a skilled manpower capable of economic exploitation of world knowledge is produced and a level of scientific awareness is developed which enables the country, or for that matter the industrial enterprise which sustains it, to be aware of world trends in advanced technology and to select from the world's repertory of knowledge those new items which are really significant for application.

These are some of the problems which underlie the consideration of science policy-allocation of resources, creativity of research effort, the balance between pure and applied science, communications systems, and the whole innovative apparatus of society.

The report, 'Science and the Policy of Governments', recommended each country to establish mechanisms for the elaboration of science policies and, on the international level, invited OECD to call a meeting of ministers responsible for science and its organization to discuss these matters further. The first ministerial meeting was held in 1963. Only a few countries had, at that time, already appointed science ministers, so that about two-thirds sent their ministers of education. The chairman of this first assembly of science ministers was the Belgian Prime Minister who was also Minister for Science. By the time the third ministerial meeting took place in 1968, most of the countries had made some special arrangements for science policy and had ministers responsible; furthermore in a number of cases science ministers were accompanied by their economics colleagues.

The ministerial discussions included the nature of science policy, how resources for science are allocated, the place of fundamental research and of the social sciences respectively in the policy of governments, the relation between research and economic growth, the function of governments in industrial innovation, and international cooperation in research.

As a basis for considering resource allocation, quantitative data are essential as in other fields. OECD has therefore given considerable attention to the collection of statistics of national expenditure on research and development both in terms of finance and of professional manpower. The data published by various countries led to some misleading comparisons because of different definitions of the various categories of research and different methods of collection and analysis of the data. As a first step, therefore, a group of experts from the OECD countries was asked to formulate a series of definitions which might be generally acceptable and to search for a uniform method of census. This was done on the basis of a first draft by a consultant and led to the compilation of the so-called Frascati Manual, which, after discussion by the statisticians of each country, was modified and finally adopted by the OECD Council as a basis for country action.

Meanwhile a careful analysis of the existing international data on R & D expenditure had been compiled by Freeman and Young and published just before the second meeting of science ministers to provide an initial comparison of national efforts. Although admittedly crude, this report did give an initial comparison of the research rescources of the United States, the Soviet Union, and the West European countries. It indicated the inferior position of the latter, even if allowance was made for the huge American expenditures on defence and space. This led ministers to question whether the disparities of research and development effort between Europe and the United States might have a deleterious influence on future economic and trade development in Europe, thus raising the question of the so-called technological gap which has aroused much political controversy, having the positive result, however, of causing ministers and industrialists in the European countries to review their scientific efforts and to make proposals for various cooperative schemes and institutional developments which might consolidate the European effort as a whole, to make it more competitive with that of the two giant powers.

The second meeting of ministers of science invited OECD to study this matter in depth, and this has given rise to many studies presented to the third ministerial meeting held in March 1968. To provide a quantitative basis, OECD declared 1964—65 to be an International Statistical Year for Research and Development. Most of the member countries gathered data on this time basis, in accordance with the methods of Frascati. Analysis of the results yielded a quantitative and comparative picture of the situation in each country which, however imperfect, gave for the first time some indication of the relative efforts of the various countries. These statistical comparisons of R & D in the OECD countries are now undertaken every two years. Work is now in progress which will result in a revision of the Frascati Manual to include the social sciences. Furthermore, work is now being undertaken to analyze the R & D effort not merely globally but with regard to the distribution of that effort between the various sectors of objective.

The studies of the technological gap which were reported to the third meeting of ministers of science were in a sense a turning point in the evolution of 'science for policy', in this case science for the economy. They indicated that the level of R & D effort of a country had little influence on its economic growth or on its performance in trade. In fact, the transfer of technology from country to country is sufficiently rapid to counteract deficiencies in the national research effort. This applies only, of course, to countries which have a research activity sufficiently high so as to be aware in detail of scientific and technological developments wherever they may have taken place in the world and a skilled manpower to utilize them. Stress is therefore given to the process of technological innovation rather than to the fundamental inputs on which it is based and which can be either indigenous or purchased from abroad. The innovation process is itself very complex and depends on many factors such as managerial skill and entrepreneurship, levels of education, availability of risk capital, fiscal policies, and, not least, marketing ability. This multivariant nature of technological innovation is increasingly seen as common to problems of initiating change in a wide variety of systems, social as well as economic.

Research cooperation through common planning
The nature of scientific activity has changed greatly in recent years, through the development of a team approach, the need for multi-disciplinary work and the multivariant nature of the problems it is called on to solve. The cost as well as the extent of research has increased greatly and in some fields of both pure and applied research, equipment and installations are beyond the means of all but the largest countries. This has led to the creation of a whole series of intergovernmental organizations for particular research fields, especially in Europe, for purposes of cost-sharing and to give the advantages of cross-fertilization which international work makes possible. On the other hand, there are many fields of both fundamental and applied research where central installations are not inherently necessary and where noninstitutionalized means of cooperation might be developed, thus avoiding the political difficulties of large international research budgets and the inherent bureaucracy of intergovernmental work.

OECD has undertaken a number of experiments to stimulate such work, especially in applied fields where the research effort of the individual countries was probably sub-threshold. Examples are marine corrosion and the biological deterioration of materials. In such cases, meetings of experts were convened in Paris from those countries interested in such cooperation, which varied from topic to topic. The objective was to create over a period common programs of experimental work, taking account of existing national effort, and to assign to each of the collaborating laboratories responsibility for particular elements of the programs. This was successfully achieved in a number of fields, and after an initial period necessary for the establishment of mutual confidence and common planning, these groups became independent international research networks working under the patronage of the Organization but without its financial contribution.

In one instance — that of road research, which is normally a governmental responsibility — the activity has been retained within OECD. For this field, which includes road construction, road and automobile safety, traffic control, etc., some 20 countries contribute to a small professional secretariat within OECD (five people only) which serves the constituent laboratories of the scheme. There is no central research fund. Work is of two types: firstly, a common information service has been created for the sector, which is extremely effective and probably gives better service to its members than could be achieved on a national basis. Furthermore, its magnetic tapes and print-offs are sold to highway authorities all over the world and contribute to the overheads. Secondly, a series of 'state of the art' groups have been created for a large number of specific problem areas in this subject, which analyse national programs, identify the major problems, make recommendations to governments, and suggest common research projects. These are undertaken by bilateral and multilateral cooperation between groups of interested laboratories by direct contribution from their own budgets and manpower without the bureaucratic difficulties normally associated with intergovernmental work. These methods of international cooperation are simple, avoid political difficulties, and might be emulated with advantage in many fields where large central equipment is not inherently necessary.

At present our research programming and implementation methods are somewhat static and lead all too easily to obsolescent institutions as priorities change, missions are accomplished, and research workers grow older. Attention needs to be given to new, flexible, dynamic, and less institutionalized methods of research programming and operation to meet the new complex of problems facing society, to the solution of which research should have much to contribute.

Science and development
The OECD countries are the main donors of aid to the developing world, and hence the Organization is strongly concerned with aid policies and with the development process. It does not, however, operate any technical assistance programs for the third world. Nevertheless, certain activities developed for the less industrialized of the member countries such as Turkey, Yugoslavia, and Portugal have proved useful in other parts of the world. This is especially the case with a series of pilot teams for technology which were set up to assess the total scientific and technological effort of particular countries, define development needs requiring technical support, and suggest how the two might be coupled. A further example was the Mediterranean Regional Project, which developed means for estimating the investments in educational resources — finance, teachers, in-

stitutions — necessary to achieve a country's long-term development objectives.

At present a survey is being made of the research activities of the member countries aimed at solving problems of development; in particular, detailed information is being assembled with regard to such efforts in a number of specific fields designated by the United Nations as of priority importance. It is hoped from such investigations to identify gaps in the total effort and to suggest areas where cooperative work between countries tackling facets of a particular problem might produce a reinforced result.

The new approach to science policy

During the decade of OECD activity on the issues of science policy, there have been great changes both in the nature of the problems which face society and to the solution of which research might contribute, and also in attitudes towards science and technology. Throughout most of the period resources for research and development were rising rapidly; it was in fact a period of scientific euphoria. In recent years, however, the value of such activities to society has been questioned, partly due to recognition of the unwanted side effects of technology, particularly through air and water pollution, and partly through a growing questioning as to the quality of life in general in a technology-dominated society. The OECD felt, in 1971, that it was timely to review the place of science and its policies in view of changing attitudes towards both economic growth and science itself and particularly with regard to the range of new problems facing society. A group of independent scientists and economists under the chairmanship of Dean Harvey Brooks was therefore invited to survey the situation, and its report issued with the title, 'Science, Growth and Society', formed the basis of a fourth meeting of science ministers held at the end of 1971. The ministers reached a consensus that research and development had contributed to society to an extent which far exceeded the undesirable effects, not only through growth of the economy and the material prosperity of the individual which this entails, but also in health, agriculture, and other fields. More and not less research was required, but national efforts should be reorientated towards new goals and particularly social goals. Science could no longer be regarded as an autonomous area of policy but should be developed in articulation with other aspects of national activity and especially social and economic policies.

The ministers defined what they felt should be the main thrusts of scientific effort and policy for the next decade. Firstly, all the member countries still had major need for economic growth, although this should not be seen as an end in itself but the means to provide the resources necessary to develop society as a whole, such as education, health care, better cities, environment, etc. Economic growth requires still more technological development and research on which this is evolved. Thus considerable research and development activity towards economic objectives is to be seen. However, the new technological developments must be socially acceptable and hence the second thrust will be to ensure the better management of technology in the interests of society as a whole. Among other things this will necessitate the development and use of means of foreseeing the effects — social and cultural as well as economic — of new and envisaged technological options: so-called technology assessment.

The third direction proposed is a more important research effort aimed at providing innovation in the service and social sectors in which existing scientific activities are still minor compared to those for defence, industry, and agriculture.

The scientific activities of OECD have been considerably reoriented as a consequence of these considerations. They include studies aimed at a better understanding of how technological innovation may be effectively stimulated, the management of technology and assessment of its probable effects, investigation of the principles governing innovation in the service sectors, policies for the social sciences and their application — all subjects of considerable complexity.

The new problems to which research must respond are inherently complex, and solutions can only be found if scientific, economic, social, and political aspects are considered together. This will mean a much greater extent of interdisciplinary contact and of 'horizontal' team work. OECD is already beginning to reorganize itself to take such approaches. For example, its comprehensive study of the world energy problem to 1985 and beyond involves research aspects and also economic, monetary, environmental, social, and political elements. The new science policy is likely to develop on similar multidisciplinary lines.

AN INTERNATIONAL RESEARCH CORPORATION — A STEP TOWARDS THE FINANCING OF THE 'FOURTH WORLD'?*

Carl-Göran Hedén, Karolinska Institutet and the Medical Research Council, Stockholm

1. *Organization as social inventions*

As earlier emphasized by Sam Nilsson, when he asked if scientists and engineers are ready for international coordination, many problems in the current world situation point to the need for unpopular solutions and long-range actions with delayed political pay-offs. This is an obstacle to development, both nationally and on the international scene, because in both cases group polarizations tend to divert Man's attention away from his basic needs. Or, phrased differently, attention is focused rather on lower order goals, where the political debate generates a clear-cut profile, than on higher order goals, which are apt to be more distant and dim. However, as shown by the independent stand now taken by some brave individuals who voice their views in the face of severe criticism, or even political persecution, the present need for non-political inputs is often felt very strongly. Nationally such inputs emerge all the way from turbulent student movements to the most illustrious academies. Internationally, on the other hand, they derive from sources as diverse as multinational corporations, labor unions, the Pugwash movement and the non-governmental organizations (NGOs) in science. I will concern myself specifically with the latter because they have a special significance which is highlighted by Karl Popper's observation that the old phrase 'noblesse oblige' should now be replaced by 'sagesse oblige'. But however strongly an individual scientist might feel his responsibility, he is powerless in a highly organized society, so the organization itself becomes 'the avenue to ... new social ethics for the conduct of science' (1). But here we face a problem, because when organizations grow they tend to petrify, so — in our times of rapid change — entirely new structures may be the essential 'social inventions'. Even so, we look at them with hesitation, which is natural for anyone burdened with much travel and committee work. Still, like Dror, I guess we realize that 'while the difficulties and dangers of problems tend to increase at a geometric rate, the knowledge and

* Paper delivered in the author's capacity as Chairman of the Liaison Committee of the International Federation of Institutes for Advanced Study (IFIAS).

91

manpower qualified to deal with these problems tend to increase with an arithmetic rate' (2). Consequently we must give a lot of attention to the question of how problems can be attacked most efficiently. An important thing is then to realize that anything that we might call a global problem is really a web of interrelated problems which may be referred to as a 'problematique'. This is not easy to comprehend because it is hard to give up the Cartesian view of the universe, with its emphasis on parts and elements, in favor of a systems approach which concentrates on wholes and patterns. However, a change in our approach is now slowly coming about, as indicated by the current science policy debate and by many new trends in university education. In fact the value of the transdisciplinary attack on major problems is now generally recognized, even if the necessary structures for the desired crossfertilization are often lacking. However, there are exceptions like the newly established non-governmental 'International Federation of Institutes for Advanced Study' (IFIAS), from which I will take the example discussed in this paper.

2. *A transnational power dimension: the Fourth World*

Much of our global thinking is geared toward a two-dimensional political pattern, which we simplify in terms like 'East', 'West' and 'The Third World'. Such terms leave little room for the transnational power dimension, which I like to call 'the Fourth World' (3). This world is singularly important, because the center of gravity within its particular hierarchy of loyalties (human, global, regional, national, local, and family) is quite different from the one we find in the other three worlds and hopefully also more prone to generate the social inventions which we now need in order to adjust to a rapidly changing physical and mental environment.

However, before the science segment of the 'Fourth World' can help the political mechanism to shift resources from short-range to long-range goals, it needs to define the proper focusing points and to develop mechanisms to bring its message across. From this point of view various disciplines have reached very different stages of preparedness. This is partly due to the fact that their relevance to practical applications varies, and partly it is because they have been forced more or less drastically into soul-searching. Seen in this perspective microbiology is a very interesting subject, not only because of its diverse social impacts in the most critical target area, the LDCs (4, 5), but also because of the activities that were needed a few years ago in order to help in the elimination of the spectre of biological weapons (6). It also deserves special attention because it lies at the core of an exceedingly important new branch of technology: enzyme engineering. Finally it is so well organized internationally that we can think of it as one of the helpful power grids of the Fourth World. Besides the UN agencies there is for instance a large International Association of Microbiological Societies (IAMS), and recently — at the 150th Anniversary of Pasteur's birth — serious talks were also initiated by IFIAS about the creation of a mission-oriented non-governmental network of microbiological laboratories. All those activities have generated and will continue to generate results which must be brought to the notice of decision-makers, and that is why a special type of Conference: the Global Impacts of Applied Micro-biology (GIAM) meetings, were started a decade ago.

3. *Science and technology in the LDCs*

The aim of the GIAM Conferences was to bring scientists and poli-ticians together for regular meetings (7, 8, 9, 10), so that they could discuss the potential of microbiology for development, primarily in the underprivileged areas of the world. Earlier this year (3) I tried to put this initiative in perspective by showing a few diagrams, one of which is Fig. 1 (p. 97). It illustrates the world of science as it ap-peared in 1967, which was the first time that a GIAM conference could be arranged in a developing country. The scientific activities that particular year have been studied by, for instance, De Solla Price (11), who used the documentation tapes which reflect the number of papers published. As you will see from the Figure, which is based on one of his diagrams, there is a rather clearcut linear relation between the publication activity and the economic size of a country. Because the latter should also reflect the technological size if looked at the number of granted patents (12) in some of the countries he had anal-yzed (big circles). However, since it normally takes some years to get a patent I actually took those figures from 1971 (lower right hand side of the diagram).

The figure indicates that the countries we should focus on — in the interest of development — are the ones where we count the num-ber of publishing scientists in the hundreds, and where less than a few thousand patents are granted every year. These are also the countries that lag behind, in the sense that they are separated from the devel-oped countries by a dangerous economic gap, which is rapidly grow-ing. This is no mystery if one considers the handicaps associated with science or engineering in such countries: a 'soft state', research posts and funding used as privileges, bad training, unqualified staff and inadequate equipment, travel restrictions, and incomplete libraries. This is no place to list all the possible remedies to this situation, but it is important to note that in the last couple of years the situation has become a priority problem not only within the UN family (ACAST, Specialized Agencies, etc.) but also among many NGOs (COSTED, IFS, IFIAS, etc.).

However, financial resources of a new magnitude are needed if we are dissatisfied with the current symptomatic treatment and want to achieve curative effects. Various schemes for raising this money have been proposed, for instance in the context of the discussions about an international legal regime for those resources of the seabed which lie beyond the limits of national jurisdiction (oil, gas, minerals, etc.). However, even if this would permit revenue sharing with the international community, it is difficult to see how it would help to close the gap between the rich and the poor countries. Other ideas, like a UN tax on international travel and transport might then be more effective and a levy related to the GNP/capita even better. But such ideas are apt to flounder in the ferment of conflicts between strong biased interests, so we should also consider systems aimed at some 'indirect tax', influencing the growth factors for development rather than the committed resources. Such a growth factor is the science and technology which can be translated into new patents, the utilization of which we could try to divert from the industrialized countries to the developing areas of the world.

4. *Patents and technology transfer*
The Atlantic Charter of 1943 and later the UN Charter (Article 55) aim for the enjoyment by all states, great or small, of access, on equal terms, to the trade and to the raw materials of the world, which are needed for their economic prosperity. With regard to equal terms between nations, however, Myrdal (13), points out that 'it is an ideal that they *should* be equal but if, in fact, they are not, equal treatment becomes inequality'. His consequent argument for double standards of morality in international trade of course also holds for technology transfer.

It has often been claimed that the economic advancement of the underprivileged areas of the world not only requires efficient instruments for the transfer of technology but also the development of new technologies, specially adapted to local problems. The former approach raises a group of problems that is a major concern of ECOSOC, UNIDO, and other intergovernmental organizations. The latter domain, on the other hand, has attracted special attention from non-governmental organizations, such as the Standing Conference on the Impact of Technology on Developing Countries (set up five years ago at Washington University), VITA (Volunteers for International Technical Assistance Inc. in the US), and the Intermediate Technology

Group Ltd. in Britain (14). As indicated by many aid programs the importance of the latter type of approach is, however, also clearly understood by most governments, and many of them may in fact be ready to consider concerted efforts that could pave the way for innovations geared to the specific needs of developing countries. They would then have to consider reward systems and the problems of coordinating such systems with the international patent legislation.

This is governed by the Paris Union or Convention, which was drawn up at a time when the problems of the developing countries were not felt as acutely as they are today, and when only benefits from an international patent system could be visualized for the LDCs. However, the need for preferential treatment of the developing countries is now quite apparent and in 1964 the UNCTAD Conference in fact accepted the principle of non-reciprocity in patent matters. The United International Bureau for the Protection of Intellectual Property (BIBPI) has also published a 'model law' which reflects similar ideas. However, Anderfelt, who has analyzed the international patent legislation and the developing countries (15), finds that the adjustment process is too slow and largely inadequate with regard to such matters as sanctions against nonworking (for instance compulsory licensing), the requirement to provide supplementary know-how, export limitations, etc. On the basis of the experience from the copyright field he advocates that the developing countries should 'display a stronger, more unified stand than they have shown so far'.

The copyright field was governed by the Berne and Inter-American Unions until 1951, when UNESCO challenged the Unions by proposing the Universal Copyright Convention. This was natural, since UNESCO is concerned with safeguarding free communication of the mind and was obliged to express concern about the availability, to developing countries, of educational publications. Its initiative forced the Berne Union into a cooperative posture, and the 1967 Revision Conference of the Union adapted a special protocol on the preferential treatment of developing countries. This attitude is also likely to influence the Paris Union, since the two Unions are connected in the 'World Intellectual Property Organization' (WIPO) established in 1967. The latter organization might eventually develop into a Specialized Agency, but it seems unlikely that ECOSOC would support such a move until many developing countries — and other members that do not belong to the original Unions — can have a stronger influence. This will certainly be a difficult problem to resolve, and a UN initiative similar to the Universal Copyright Convention might act as a powerful accelerator. In discussing such a move

Anderfelt (15) feels that a 'Universal Patent Convention' would be a realistic proposal. It would be a system for patent cooperation 'with a principle based on the needs of various groups of countries including the acceptance of preferential treatment for developing countries'. However, he also emphasizes that changes in the present international patent system should be supplemented with other measures like a 'World Fund of Technological Knowledge'.

5. A 'World Fund of Technological Knowledge'
Actually the establishment of an international Clearing House function for technical documentation and know-how is often considered in UN documents (16, 17, 18, 19). Subscription to such a fund, by the industrialized countries, could be made either through funds that could be employed to buy technology in the market or by pledging the rights to patent-protected inventions to the fund. Anderfelt (15) visualizes that the second approach would involve subscription to the fund of all patents originally granted by a country, but he realizes that such a scheme would be more strongly opposed than the former. However, he also points out that between half and two-thirds of all R & D funds are supplied by Governments, and that it has often been suggested that there should be free international disclosure of industrial technology developed by public research agencies (20, 21).

6. An 'International Research Corporation' — an exploratory NGO initiative
It is obvious that a fund, such as that outlined, could be used to remunerate inventors contributing to the economic growth of developing countries, but it could also sponsor desirable contract research. It might also establish highly competent resource development or know-how teams, circulate lists of 'problems in search of solutions', establish an international employment agency for specialists, etc. Indeed, there is no lack of obvious needs that should catch the eyes of many non-governmental organizations that might wish to prepare the ground for major intergovernmental activities. One such exploratory initiative could be an International Research Corporation based on patents granted to individual scientists, engineers, and other inventors, who might want to see part of their royalty income being used for the benefit of the underprivileged parts of the world. Two major questions relate to such a project: 1. Would it be possible to raise the initial funding to a level above which the activities would be self-propelling? 2. What would be the response of the individual inventor? Given the necessary administrative and financial support, and knowing that their efforts would contribute to the global de-

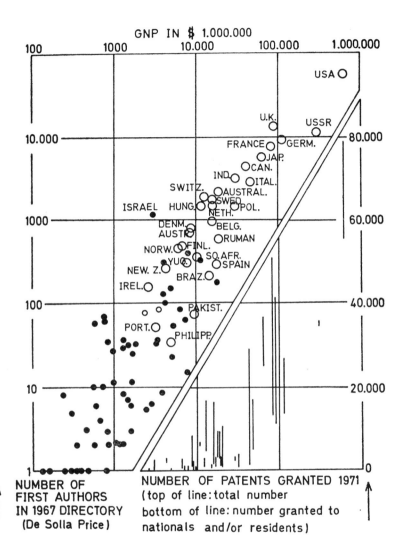

GNP IN $ 1.000.000

NUMBER OF
FIRST AUTHORS
IN 1967 DIRECTORY
(De Solla Price)

NUMBER OF PATENTS GRANTED 1971
(top of line: total number
bottom of line: number granted to
nationals and/or residents)

velopment process, would scientists for instance patent their products and processes to a larger extent than they do now?

With regard to the first question it should be realized that many sources could be tapped, ranging from the most altruistic Foundations to major business corporations that currently only think in terms of future markets and consider present-day economic assistance primarily as a means to increase future world prosperity. Even National Research Corporations and Commercial Contract Research Organizations might find it advantageous to become founding members, because many of them certainly sense the wind of change, and 'no legal system can protect itself except by providing adequate scope for evolutionary change' (22). Obviously then, the possibilities to raise the necessary funds should not be too hopeless, at least if a solid case — based on some practical results — could be presented.

With regard to the second question, concerning the response of individuals, the answer of course depends on two factors: the strength of their wish to contribute to global development and their legal freedom to do so. Since the normal professional activities of scientists and engineers is intimately related to human progress and economic development, however, it is likely that the response would be more favorable than that of a general population cross-section. Above a certain activity threshold of a concerted program the concern for development and technology transfer might even become part of the professional ethos and a snowballing effect could occur. Many scientists would then cease to frown at the practice of patenting inventions made in the course of research work. However, the actual level of such an activity threshold is impossible to estimate without some practical experience.

7. Transdisciplinary research cooperation in enzyme engineering — an experiment in guiding major efforts toward global development and human welfare

The logical conclusion of the above considerations is that there is a need for a transdisciplinary experiment which, if successful, might serve as a first step toward the creation of an International Research Corporation. This experiment should then take the form of a grant application concerning a project within a well-defined field of obvious significance to the future of the developing countries, and there could be few more suited than enzyme engineering. The response of the granting agencies to such an application would, in itself, be a part of the experiment, particularly if the motor fund eventually needed was made conditional upon the attainment of a certain minimum level of exploitable patents deriving from the first lot of proposals.

In fact the experiment mentioned has already started in the process of securing suitable proposals for such an effort. IFIAS, for instance, has been able to evaluate the response of scientists at a number of round-table meetings where various measures relating to royalties and licensing have been discussed. One suggestion, for instance, was that the inventor would get 25 percent of the royalties and guide the distribution of another 25 percent to his co-workers, assistants, institution, etc., whereas a final 50 percent would be added to a motor fund that could be used for further research and technology transfer aimed at the underprivileged areas of the world.

With regard to licensing the following sentence was considered for inclusion in the research proposals:

> It is understood that licensing of inventions developed within the framework of this proposal will aim at stimulating use in developing countries. Exclusive licenses on patent(s) deriving from this study will consequently be avoided, and the license fees will be related to the GNP/capita of the country whose citizens control more than 50 percent of the shares in the company that will execute the invention(s).

An unexpected and remarkable outcome of those discussions, which have involved some 50 eminent specialists from all over the world, is that nobody so far has raised serious objections of principle, and that many specialists expressed strong interest in the effort and a wish to submit proposals. As a consequence the following project parcel will be submitted for consideration to IFIAS at the next Board Meeting (Paris, Oct. 15—17, 1973):

A. The use of enzyme engineering for environmental control and energy management.
  a. A biochemical system for the continuous monitoring of the environment.
  b. Enzymes as penetration aids for insect pathogens.
  c. Biochemical fuel cell systems.
  d. Biochemical hydrogen generation.

B. The use of enzyme engineering for improving medical care.
  a. A miniaturized clinical analysis system for use in multiphase health testing.
  b. Microencapsulated one-shot vaccines.

c. Studies on the possible uses of antibodies as guided missiles for enzymes and enzyme inhibitors.

C. Studies on methods that might be used for large-scale preparation of syntehtic enzymes.

However, the variations in the legal practice of various institutions is great, so the proposals cannot always include passages as specific as those mentioned earlier. To be accepted as part of the experiment they must, however, at least contain the following statement:

> The investigator is aware of IFIAS' wish to use its project on transdisciplinary research cooperation on enzyme engineering as an experiment in the search for methods to guide research efforts towards global development and human welfare. In securing patents and in making licensing agreements the interests of the economically underpreviledged areas of the world will consequently be given special consideration.

8. *Conclusion*

A systematic transdisciplinary research cooperation in enzyme technology might well generate attractive products with a great potential impact on health, environmental management, and manufacturing techniques. This means that we consider an R & D area that is rapidly becoming 'hot', in the sense that it is starting to attract industrial interest. However, many industrial empires (at least outside Japan) have not yet adjusted to the fact that 'the future belongs to biology'. They in fact seem to lack the overview and competence, and possibly also the imagination, to commit biologists to their goals as efficiently as they have done in areas like physics, electronics, and metallurgy. Whatever the reason, enzyme engineering could be an area where the scientific segment of the Fourth World might have an edge over the industrial. At least this is true if we consider applications which require large inputs of basic research like industrial biosynthesis, biochemical fuel cells, and biochemical nitrogen fixation. Systematic, well-coordinated studies in such fields might well generate patents that could be of very great significance to the developing countries, for whom the international patent system has been a rather mixed blessing so far. If successful, a concerted action might provide a starting point for an 'International Research Corporation' that could eventually form the basis for a UN 'World Fund of Technological Knowledge' — a structure that might be of fundamental importance for the technology transfer needed by the developing parts of the world.

REFERENCES

(1) Collins, F., at Conference on Social Responsibility of Scientists, arranged by N.Y.Acad.Sci. and reviewed in *The Sciences*, p. 8, Jan.—Feb. 1972.

(2) Dror, Yehezkel, 'Protegomenon to political sciences: from muddling through to metapolicy making'. *Symp. on Policy Sciences*. AAAS-meeting. Boston. 1969.

(3) Hedén, C.-G., 'Man and the Microbiosphere». *Proc.Conf.on Global Impacts of Applied Microbiology*. Sao Paulo, July 22—28, 1973 (in press).

(4) Hedén, C.-G., Potential of applied microbiology. *Ann.N.Y. Acad.Sci. 184*, 113, 1971.

(5) Hedén, C.-G., Invitation lecture: 'Applied microbiology — for life or for death'. 3rd International Conference on Global Impacts of Applied Microbiology. Bombay, Dec. 7—12, 1969. University of Bombay, 1971.

(6) Hedén, C.-G., 'A professional verdict over BW'. *New Scientist*, 10 Sept. 1970, p. 518—520.

(7) 1st International Conference: *Global Impacts of Applied Microbiology*. Ed.: M. P. Starr, Stockholm, July 29 to Aug. 3, 1958. Almqvist & Wiksell, Stockholm, and John Wiley & Sons, Inc., New York, 1964.

(8) 2nd International Conference: *Global Impacts of Applied Microbiology*. Ed.: E. L. Gaden, Jr., Addis Ababa, Nov. 6—11, 1967. Interscience Publishers, New York, 1969.

(9) 3rd International Conference: *Global Impacts of Applied Microbiology*. Eds.: Y. M. Freitas and F. Fernandes. Bombay, Dec. 7—12, 1969. University of Bombay. 1971.

(10) 4th International Conference: *Global Impacts of Applied Microbiology*. Sao Paulo, July 22—28, 1973. (In press).

(11) De Solla Price, D. J., Measuring the size of science. *Proc. Israel Acad.Sci. Human 4*, 98, 1969.

(12) Patent applications filed and patents granted during 1971 — an extract from a world table published in the Dec. 1972 issue of *Industrial Property*, the monthly review of the World Intellectual Property Organization. *IFIA Bull.*, p.iii, 1973.

(13) Myrdal, G., An International Economy. Routledge & Kegan Paul, London 1956.

(14) Schumacher, E. F., A plea for intermediate technology. *Ceres FAO Review 1*, 29, 1968.

(15) Anderfelt, U., *The International Patent Legislation and Developing Countries*. Martinus Nijhoff, The Hague 1971.

(16) *UN. Doc. E/C 5/51*. Jan. 21, 1964, par. 1.

(17) Operative paragraph 4 of recommendation A.IV. 26. *Doc. E/Conf. 46/141*. Vol. 1, 3rd Part Annexes. UNCTAD 1964.

(18) Operative paragraph 1 of *ECOSOC Res. 1013* (XXXVII), July 22, 1964.

(19) Operative paragraph 3 of *UN Ass. Resolution 2091* (XX), Dec. 20, 1965.

(20) Terrill, R. T., Cartels and the international exchange of technology. *A.E.R. 36*, 762 ff. May 1946.

(21) Mason, E. S., *Controlling World Trade: Cartels and Commodity Agreements*. McGraw-Hill, New York 1946.

(22) Jenks, W. C., *The Common Law of Mankind*. Stevens, London 1958.

THE USES OF EARTH SATELLITES

J. E. S. Fawcett, London

The use of Earth satellites illustrates some of the problems of the international coordination of science and technology, and their application to development, though it is not of course wholly representative. But it brings out an important point, which must be stressed at once, about international coordination. It is this: activities which are global in extent or in their social and environmental impact, create global problems; but it does not follow that there are or even can be unitary solutions or arrangements on the same global scale, though there may be techniques applicable in many parts of the world. The pursuit of a global solution may be wholly misleading, and regional arrangements, themselves involving inevitably much international collaboration, are often to be preferred as being both easier to achieve and more likely to succeed. Alternatively, action may be usefully taken at two levels: for example, a global approach through the declaration or adoption of general principles and standards by the UN General Assembly or one of the specialized agencies, and regional arrangements implemented through national action in particular countries. So the use of Earth satellites is global in extent; for they ring the Earth with incomparable speed and are 'visible' to vast regions, so that their impact and potential value cross all frontiers. But satellite operations need technological sophistication, the investment of much capital, and the application of extended industrial resources, so that only a handful of countries can undertake them in the coming years; further, the most effective and economic use of satellites is likely to be through regional or partial satellite systems, governed nevertheless by certain general rules on the use of orbital and radio resources.

We may then survey first the dynamics of space operations, and then their necessary international coordination.

But first the uses of Earth satellites must be briefly described. A distinction has come to be made between 'application satellites' and those devoted to scientific investigation, but it may be more convenient here to divide their functions into communications, surveys, and transport.

As instruments of communication satellites provide telecommunication services in the form of radio and telephone messages, and radio and TV broadcasting, and data distribution, in the forms, for example, of air and sea navigation 'fixes' and stock market prices. By one of the agreements of May 1972 between the US and USSR, emergency exchanges between Washington and Moscow can now be made through a telecommunication satellite. Further, telecommunication satellites may be instruments of air traffic control, marine navigation, and weapons control, as well as serving as vehicles for education, information, and persuasion.

The survey functions of satellites are primarily scientific though some are directed to practical needs. Surveys of the upper atmosphere, combined with cloud surveys and atmospheric measurements, constitute the World Weather Watch, established in 1964 and elaborated by the WMO (World Meteorological Organization) in 1967. Surveys by satellite of Earth resources, particularly sea fish stocks and mineral deposits on land, are now being developed, account being taken of pollution traces and environmental changes. There are also the highly sophisticated surveillance satellites, operated by both the US and the USSR, keeping continuous watch over strategic areas and movements.

Transport by satellite, or for the servicing of satellites in orbit, is still to come, but the space station has already been in operation, and the NASA plans for a space shuttle are well advanced.

II

In the dynamics of satellite operations we may observe two influential factors: the thrust of technology, and cooperation and conflict between the operators.

Research and development behind space technology have over the last two decades depended on a massive financial input by governments, in which defence interests have had a great part. This investment has been abnormal in the sense that it has carried production far beyond what industrial investors would contemplate or the market justify without such support. So the 'lives' of particular types of satellites have, as the evolution of INTELSAT I–IV of the International Telecommunications Satellite Consortium shows, been progressively shortened by the pressure at each stage of the new product, and the increasing cost of this partly artificial growth enable only the largest enterprises — outside the US and USSR, usually transnational consortia — to carry on.[1] There is then a concentration of industrial power and science and technology resources, in a small number of areas and a few hands, in which production for marketing still dominates, there are secrecy and competition, and governmental agencies, such as NASA and the Office of Management and Budget in the US, are involved sometimes in cooperation and sometimes in conflict with the major enterprises. This is well illustrated by the efforts to introduce international air traffic control by satellite over the North Atlantic and the Pacific. PanAm had tested aircraft-satellite communication in 1964, and BOAC had carried out ground tests in 1967. ASTRA (Application of Space Techniques Relating to Aviation), a technical panel set up by ICAO in 1968, recommended the use of frequencies from 1535—1660 Mhz in view of the ever-growing demands on the radio spectrum. In August 1971 agreement was reached between ESRO and the US Federal Aeronautics Administration on a pre-operational 'aerosat' program. It envisaged a sophisticated six-satellite system using the recommended frequencies and providing air traffic control for the North Atlantic and Pacific, at an estimated cost of $245 million. Conflict developed at two points, budgetary and technical. The US Office of Management and Budget and other governmental agencies intervened against the implementation of the scheme on ground of cost, and a reduced scheme using three satellites at a cost of $90 million was proposed in January 1973. But this did not wholly answer the second and technical objection, made by the airlines, that the 'aerosat' plan for traffic control was more sophisticated and costly than was needed. Ordinary high frequency communication (3—30 Mhz) without access to satellites was proving, for a number of reasons, to be better able to provide the means of traffic control than had been earlier believed, and in fact four extra channels were given to air traffic control in the North Atlantic at the end of 1971. Among the reasons were improved diminution of the frequency band-width used and the relative reduction of flights, larger aircraft now carrying more passengers and cargo.

Two lessons may perhaps be drawn, one for the industrialized countries where satellite operations are concentrated, and the other for developing countries. In the former, greater Parliamentary knowledge and intervention are needed to control satellite developments, by forcing the issues of policy, both technological and commercial, into public debate, by reducing wasteful and unnecessary conflicts between governments and enterprises, and by resolving the issues of public and private ownership of satellite resources. Satellites may be prestigious, but unduly expensive, in money and resources. So oceanic cables have remained fully competitive with Earth satellites for telephone communications, and both sounding rockets and highaltitude balloons can perform a number of Earth or atmosphere surveys as efficiently as satellites and certainly more cheaply. Developing countries might then take note that, however prestigious home production of satellite equipment may be, a more cautious and in the end better investment of domestic resources is in the ability to service equipment, hired or purchased from abroad.

III

The necessary international coordination of Earth satellite operations extends over a number of areas: the allocation of two natural resources, orbital space and frequency bands; copyright; commercial use; surveys; and uses for information, education, and persuasion.

To see what part the UN system can play, we may look at the first and last two.

The Intelsat system was reorganized in May 1971 after years of difficult negotiation. Three features of its structure, as built in 1964, were causes of discontent to many of the eighty countries participating in it. First, Comsat (Communication Satellite Corporation)[2] was manager, but as a US corporation was subject, in awarding contracts in the United States, to the jurisdiction of the Federal Communication Commission, whose approval, for example, had to be obtained from the grant of the INTELSAT III contract even after decision of the international Intelsat Committee. Secondly, since shares in the corporation were held in substantial part by its potential competitors,[3] they could have an unbalancing influence in its directing board. Thirdly, too much procurement had been concentrated in the United States and too little subcontracting in participating countries; though this could be attributed in part to the fact that specialized subcontracting is more highly developed and so more cost-efficient than outside. Finally, Intelsat has no control over the prices which common telecommunication carriers charge for services using satellite channels. High rates can be imposed then to subsidize ordinary domestic services, or profits withheld which might otherwise go to reduce the cost of satellite operations. Whether the reform of Intelsat will meet or cure these defects remains to be seen. There is still to be a transitional period of six years before international management is fully substituted for that by Comsat. But Intelsat, itself an amalgam of public and private enterprises, illustrates some of the problems of international coordination of Earth Satellites that must arise in the UN System.[4]

The UN itself has acted as a forum for the establishment of common standards in the uses of outer space, through the General Assembly and COPUOS (Committee on Peaceful Uses of Outer Space), as a centre for the exchange and distribution of information, and in particular the registration of satellite launchings, and as a sponsor of launching ranges. Three divisions of the UN Secretariat are concerned directly or indirectly with space operations, and COPUOS runs, in addition to it Legal Subcommittee and Scientific and Technical Subcommittee, three Working Groups on Navigational, Direct Broadcasting, and Remote Sensing Satellites. The Committee has prepared three conventions, the most recent concerning international liability for damage caused by space objects.

However, it is the UNDP and the specialized agencies ITU, ICAO, IMCO, FAO, WHO, and UNESCO that have the most involvement and influence in the uses of Earth satellites. ITU has been well described by Professor Abram Chayes as a 'constellation of plenary bodies' rather than a unitary authority; and it exemplifies the difficulty of vertical regulation of space operations, greater even than that of reaching horizontal agreements between governments or enterprises. While the allocation of orbital space to, or 'parking', geostationary satellites is a matter of fairly simple regulation by international agreement, the allocation of radio frequencies is far more complicated and troublesome. The International Frequency Registration Board, an organ of ITU, is composed of five experts, each serving in his individual capacity. It has a number of functions, which constitute the Board neither as a passive registration office nor as an active regulatory body, and it lies somewhere between the two. It recommends, applying technical criteria, the allocation of particular frequency bands for military, commercial, scientific, and other uses; and it records the assignments of frequencies by national authorities within the bands allocated. The registration of an assigned frequency gives the national authority a prior claim to its use, and while the IFRB mediates in disputes over harmful interference between frequencies, it has no power to order discontinuance of use of frequency once registered, though it is causing interference or even though it is no longer being used. What is needed, if the expanding use of Earth Satellites is to be integrated with all the other demands on the radio spectrum, is a reform of ITU with better coordination of the consultative committees, more interventions by the plenipotentiary conference, and full regulatory powers in the IFRB.

UNESCO and ITU are cooperating in the study of the use of satellites in Latin America in the cause of culture and education, and CORUOS organized a panel meeting in India on Satellite Instructional Television Systems[5] in December 1972; the panel was able to observe at close quarters the planning and hardware of the Indian satellite instructional television experiment (SITE) organized in collaboration with the United States. The panel reported in particular the critical importance of the choice of frequencies.

The potentialities of satellite broadcasting through community receiver or perhaps later in the next decade direct into home receivers are being actively studied by UNESCO and COPUOS. The former has issued a declaration of guiding principles[6] and a COPUOS Working Group has produced a detailed report, account being taken of proposals presented by the USSR, in the form of a draft international convention, and by Canada and Sweden jointly, in the form of a draft UN General Assembly declaration of principles.[7] The prospects of direct satellite broadcasting, as a medium of information and persuasion, have prompted some governments at least to urge restraints upon it. How realistic proposals for an international code of regulation of satellite broadcasting are is questionable, and it may be asked whether common standards might more effectively be established by agreement between broadcasting authorities.

FAO is sponsoring Earth resource surveys by satellite, covering land, water, soil, fisheries, and pests, while WHO obtains information from surveys of flora changes, which may point up the distribution of locusts and other pests, and of air and water quality. These projects are part of the UN Development Program and are supported from its Special Fund. ICAO, as already described, is concerned with the possibilities of air traffic control by satellite, while IMCO and ESRO are seeking to develop maritime communication satellites.

In sum, the UN system is already much involved in the management and use of Earth Satellites but some large problems await international solution through it: the harmonization of partial satellite systems of Canada, Japan, and perhaps Europe, in addition to the Intelsat and Intersputnik[8] systems already established, and the regulation for political and social purposes of direct satellite broadcasting. If the greatest common benefit is to be obtained from Earth satellites, governments must face the demands for policy choices and institutional reforms, and, together with the space and communications enterprises, the need for sensible and enduring collaboration which they have so far not fully met.

NOTES
1 e.g. MESH (Engins Matra: Entwicklungsring Nord: SAAB: Hawker Siddeley) for the proposed air traffic system; and six French and German corporations for the SYMPHONIE satellite.
2 Created by Act of the US Congress in 1962.
3 e.g. ATT; IT and T; General Telephone; RCA; Electronics Corporation.
4 See generally UN Doc.: A/AC 105/100 'Space Activities and Resources', June 1972.

5 Report in UN Doc. A/AC 105/114, 28.3.1973.
6 UN Doc. A/AC 105/109, 15.2.1973.
7 UN Doc. A/AC 105/117, 22.6.1973.
8 In November 1971, the agreement setting up the Intersputnik organization, which had lain in draft since 1968, was concluded between Bulgaria, Cuba, Czechoslovakia, the German Democratic Republic, Hungary, Mongolia, Poland, Romania, and the USSR.

SUMMARY OF THE DISCUSSION
by
Finn Sollie

The Fridtjof Nansen Foundation at Polhøgda,
Norway

Called to discuss the subject 'coordination in the field of science and technology — the role of the specialized agencies of UN' the Symposium approached its subject essentially as a problem of mobilizing scientific research and technological development toward the solution of those major problems which mankind is facing today, viz. the international food shortage and declining resources, underdevelopment, population growth, pollution, etc. The discussion was to concentrate generally on broad political issues and on science and technology as an integrated part of the total range of man's activities rather than as a separate 'field'.

If any single statement or remark can be quoted to indicate the tone and atmosphere of the discussion, it must be one made by Norman Borlaug when he described to the Symposium the organization, work and current results of the magnificent effort known as the Green Revolution. At one point he remarked, 'The present world food shortage does not mean that population has outgrown our capacity to grow food. It means that we have made some mistakes in planning. Some horrible mistakes'. The awareness of pressing world problems and the realization that to a large extent those problems have emerged as a result of poor and inefficient planning was apparently widely shared. The general tone, however, was optimistic, because when problems exist as a result of insufficient planning and improper management rather than as a result of limitations built in by nature, there is still an opportunity to introduce change and improve the situation. Science and technology, therefore, were looked upon as tools of improvement and, not surprisingly, as was true for the papers, much of the discussion also came to be a search for new approaches and new possibilities, particularly to alleviate the problems of the developing nations. Essentially reformist in nature, this approach caused the participants to ask for possible means of influencing the development, and during the last stages much of the discussion concentrated on the possibility of setting down conclusions or recommendations as a statement from the Symposium.

Ten papers — all of which are included in this volume — were introduced to the Symposium and three oral presentations were made. Papers generally were presented two at a time at the beginning of each session, to be followed by some two hours of discussion among the participants. The order of the papers was arranged so that the discussion started from a basis of general background issues and moved through broad organizational issues toward the more specific in concrete examples: From an analysis of basic needs for an international science policy (Gottmann) and political issues and problems of coordination (Sollie), the presentation moved on to theoretical analysis and the application of models (Tinbergen). Then followed a presentation of IFIAS as an example of cooperation between institutes for advanced study (Nilsson) and a review of the role of the UN Family in relation to science and technology (Gresford). Next came an evaluation of the role of science and scientists in international development (Buzzati-Traverso) and of the application of science and technology to direct international development (Seaborg). Activities of OECD (King) and of NATO (Randers) in regard to science and technology were reviewed, a proposal for an international research corporation was made (Hedén) and three existing examples of international cooperation were presented: the theoretical physics centre in Trieste (Salam), the Green (or Wheat) Revolution (Borlaug) and the use of earth satellites (Fawcett).

Following the presentation of the papers by Gottmann and Sollie, *Gardner* opened the discussion by re-emphasizing two main factors that had been pointed out as inherent difficulties in the development of an international science policy and international coordination in science and technology. These were (1) that while the world is one unit (space-ship Earth) in a scientific sense and in terms of environment, in political terms it is divided into a multiple complex of nation states and (2) the existence of an international industrial complex where scientific research and technological development are carried out by private firms in a system of economic competition. To these he would add a third set of inherent difficulties, namely (3) those resulting from the structure of government institutions and their functioning at the national and international level. He indicated four areas where present organization of government gave rise to problems that must be overcome through restructuring of functions, powers and responsibilities:

(a) the functional system of portfolio government and sector specialization in national governments, as well as at the international level with specialized agencies with no effective central control and policy coordination;

(b) the separation of policy-making and budgetary procedures through separate sets of institutions with little or no effort at coordination;

(c) the lack of proportion at the international level between decision-making power (the one nation one vote rule) and real economic and political power and responsibility that caused some states to bypass the international organization by financing voluntary funds and programs, thus compounding the problem of international coordination;

(d) the lack of coordination between UN programs and programs and activities and similar activities of regional organizations such as OECD, ECE and NATO. It would be necessary to consider the need for coordination of UN and non-UN agencies and, in this connection even internal coordination of national governments must be considered because much of the fractionalization that can be seen at the international level reflects failure to coordinate national programs and policies.

Hedén, who gained his experience primarily from work as a scientist and non-governmental organizations, noted that in addition to such changes as might be required in government organization, a most important task would be to ensure the best possible use of already available manpower. Here, improvements might be initiated even without waiting for such political initiatives as were no doubt needed. As an example, he referred to the great number of microbiologists who had become unemployed as a result of cuts in biological weapons development in the US and whose talents could have been used for vital research in or for developing countries. Such situations indicated a need for arrangements either to bring available scientists into contact with jobs they could perform or to bring problems on which research was needed to the attention of scientists. He suggested that an international 'employment agency' for scientists might be helpful and also that by defining relevant problems where scientific research was needed and preparing lists of 'problems in search for solution' it might be possible to persuade institutions to increase their efforts in regard to just such problems.

Buzzati-Traverso deplored the deterioration in ethics among scientists, who had, in his opinion, allowed themselves to be corrupted by power, money and position and who had accepted secrecy in science and worked for group interests without regard to the high ideals of science. Responsibility for the appearance of the modern world, he said, in the words of Solzhenitsyn, rests solely in the hands of the scientists and it is up to them to reconsider their role and function and to make it compatible with the very survival of the human species which was now being threatened by impending crisis. The whole situation, he found, could be demonstrated in the following theorem:

— Science is universal in the sense that its discoveries are equally valid under the most diverse political circumstances —

— Scientific discoveries lead to applications of various kinds, in the form of technologies —

— Even the most humane technologies may become dangerous when indiscriminately applied or when used for exploitation and destruction —

— Careless technologies, exploitation and destruction are all made possible because men are loyal to the specific interests of nation states, parochial ideologies and professional clans —

— Because scientific activities, and especially technological development, are in fact sponsored by and carried out to satisfy national or private group interests, further expansion of science under the present system is incompatible with human survival —

— Further development in science, therefore, is incompatible with the continued existence of nation states —

— Mankind must choose either to stop the further development of science or to eliminate nation states directing the development and application of science —

— Scientists, who carry within themselves the perishable values of science and are an essential part of the culture of man, must refuse support for their activities unless it comes from genuine international agencies, and they must become missionaries for world government.

Tinbergen pointed out that politics is not a separate function or an autonomous force, but rather a process that can and must be influenced by other forces in society. In this context, two aspects of political activity were important: first, that political activity is based almost exclusively upon short-term interests and that there is often a clear conflict between them and the long-term interests which are not taken sufficiently into account, and, second, that there is always a wide gap between political promises and political performance. One message that must be brought to the attention of politicians was that of the clash between short-term and long-term interests and a second was that science must be applied toward the solution of a number of long-term tasks and problems. Referring to a remark by Sollie on the need to 'depolitize' problems, he mentioned international trade as a typical example of an area where scientists could contribute to 'depolitizing' the issues by applying their methods. Because until now technologies had been developed to meet the specific needs and requirements of the rich countries, he found it particularly important that technological research be oriented toward the world as a whole, taking also the poor countries into account. The totality of problems and the interrelation of their elements must be made clear.

Hambro, on the basis of his experience as a politician and diplomat, agreed that political activity was concentrated on acute problems and that long-term planning was difficult. A major difficulty, he found, was that the necessary 'messages' about long-term developments did not get through to the politicians. They were ignorant about vital problems and questions because they did not get the necessary information in a way which they could understand. Also, he emphasized, the principle of national sovereignty as built into international theory and practice represented a major danger to international cooperation. By referring to sovereignty, politicians and diplomats had a strong weapon against any international development that they did not want.

Blix, on the contrary, felt that sovereignty might not be such a decisive hindrance and, in regard to Tinbergen's emphasis on the need to serve long-term interests, he noted that lawyers, including international lawyers, had an interest in long-term results similar to that of the scientists and that the two groups therefore might be able to cooperate. In his opinion, the basic problem was a question of how one could best apply the available resources of science and technology to the major problems before us and to prevent their use for wasteful and unnecessary tasks. To do this it would be necessary, first, to identify those major problems where research and development were required and, second, to discuss measures that would ensure application of the required resources to just those problems.

King, while finding that Buzzati-Traverso's theorem would probably be right in the end, thought that any ideal solution would lie far into the future. A great deal of institutional innovation would be needed and at the international level experiments would have to be made to bypass the difficulties presented by sovereignty and national jealousies. Efforts so far, he felt, had not been effective. For instance, the interdepartmental committees set up in many countries to ensure coordination often proved to be groupings of vested interests and unable to formulate overall policies. There being no central responsibility, planning functions were split between a variety of agencies, while those who were concerned with financial decisions were still compelled to allocate money on economy grounds rather than on policy grounds and had to do so even without means or possibilities for evaluating the results of their allocations. One result of the lack of coherent national policies was that each country also failed to coordinate its own policy in the various international agencies, thus compounding the problem of international coordination. The result was that government so often had the quality of emergency approach and crisis management which, moreover, was also a result of the political 'life-span' of usually four years dictated by election periods, while the cycle of discovery and application in technological development would be 15—20 years. In spite of these difficulties, however, it was quite obvious that international 'regimes' were needed in several areas, such as for the oceans, with regard to energy, raw materials, global environment and population.

Fawcett felt that it was an illusion to think of problems as being global in scale and that it would be necessary to look toward regional solutions which would also make the whole question of coordination more manageable. *Tinbergen,* while agreeing that most problems are either regional or national in scale and must be solved on that scale, nevertheless found that there are also a few important problems that are truly global and call for global solutions, e.g. the ocean question, financial transfer from rich to poor countries, environment, etc. A second point made by *Fawcett* was that it would be wrong to consider science as *one* thing and scientists as *one* group. Scientists, too, are divided into a variety of groups, even for political and financial reasons. Consequently, the question of coordination in science and technology is in the end a political problem, the dilemma here being that while the area of government action and the need for coordination is so much wider than before, the actual powers and possibilities for government to take action are less than before.

Kristensen, too, found that scientists in the various diciplines had great difficulty in understanding each other and that this made coordination of work in several diciplines extremely difficult. In this connection he felt that a warning must be given against using the methods of mathematics and natural science in dealing with social problems. Such simplifications as were needed to present problems in models would involve gross distortions, and verbal presentation rather than mathematical equations is required to describe complicated social relationships. Also, he pointed out, the use of verbal presentation would facilitate understanding and coordination between disciplines. *Tinbergen* agreed that verbal presentation was necessary in the early reconnaissance period of scientific investigation, but maintained that measurements and quantitative methods must be also applied to solve problems in socio-economic relations, and that the results must then be translated back into verbal presentation to the public.

Dahl suggested that the present-day problem was to a large extent a cultural, perhaps psychological question quite as much as one about 'problem management'. Thirty or forty years ago there were basic needs that must be met and then it was possible to identify the problems that must be solved. Today, however, all basic needs have been filled in the rich countries and it is no longer possible to focus on the 'right problems'. At the present stage of development artificially raised expectations rather than needs are the problem, and models, such as suggested by Tinbergen, are often used to find the right kind of promises. The question, therefore, is rather one of how to select or choose subjects for development than one of identifying problems. The whole question is one of choice and not of identification.

Borlaug pointed out that all underdeveloped areas have a very real food problem and that while agriculture still employs some 70—80 percent of their manpower, food production has seldom been given a high order of priority in those countries. In those countries, there is often an overabundance of plans for development, but implementation is lacking both because the plans do not attack the right problems and because the science and technology in aid programs is over-sophisticated for countries that have no trained manpower. At the same time plans are missing in areas where they should be applied, for instance in keeping sufficient reserve stocks of food to meet crisis situations. Here, however, exporting countries do not want to keep large stockpiles for national and political reasons, while poor countries, for economic as well as political reasons are not able to meet their own needs by laying up stores.

Mera suggested that any effort in scientific research and techno-logical development had three stages: that of selecting the topic for research, that of developing the best approach to the problem and that of applying the scientific results. The real difficulty, he felt, lay in the final stage of application. In this respect, scientists would indeed be able to influence political decisions and attitudes could be changed if the right information were presented in the right way. The environment issue, he felt, was an example of how scientists can contribute in this respect.

Randers felt little optimism about the contribution international organizations might make toward improving and promoting science and technology. One could not get around the fact that we live in a world of nation states, nor could it be denied that scientists were inclined to work in fields and on problems that were of particular interest to them. For the scientists the problem was that money, which was a primary concern for their work, was controlled by national governments. He did not think that international research institutions were needed, nor that problems could be solved at the global level and the only real task of international cooperation in science must be to reduce the difficulties created by national units for proper scientific work. Problems indeed vary from region to region and underdeveloped countries have different difficulties from the developed countries. A clear distinction should be made between the task of improving science and cooperation in science on the one hand and, on the other hand, improving social conditions in developing countries. Pure science, he found, had no direct relations to social conditions.

Hedén did not agree that science could be thus set apart and argued that new approaches were indeed needed. For one thing, a number of problems can be studied only in the developing countries, where the problems are, and this would require new facilities to be created through international cooperation. Also, the kind of intermediary, rather than advanced technology that developing countries need can only be developed by exposing scientists to the needs and the situation in those countries.

King agreed with Randers that improving social conditions in the developing countries was to a large extent a humanistic, rather than a purely scientific approach, but he was also convinced that scientists are socially concerned and that they, like himself, would like to see more work concerning developing countries.

Tinbergen noted that while it is true that pure science will very often have no direct bearing upon social affairs, there are also numerous cases in which scientific work and the improvement of social condition of poor countries — as well as of rich countries — are closely related. As an example, he mentioned the task of finding a better division of labour between rich and poor countries.

Commenting upon the papers of Gresford, Buzzati-Traverso and Seaborg, *Gardner* found that we are groping for new instruments for the use of science and technology for human betterment. The paradox in this connection was that while quite impressive international networks were developing between scientific and professional men who were dedicated to the spaceship Earth concept and to international cooperation, nation states appeared to follow ever more nationalistic policies. It would be necessary therefore to establish procedures by which independent scientific evaluations and judgments could be presented regularly to governments for action. One possibility might be to apply an international parallel to the Environment Impact Statement in the US, to the effect that before undertaking actions that would have an environmental impact beyond its national borders, a state would be obliged to report this to all countries concerned, consult with them and, if necessary, accept conciliation. He further suggested that international action plans might be prepared that called for goals and targets to be set by national governments and that such plans might start a process of planning in various countries. He also noted that the existing networks between scientists have so far developed on a sectoral basis while there should be an overall system, such as an international Commission on the Future.

Gresford, referring to the emphasis put on the problems of developing countries in the papers and in the discussion, stressed the need to consider the wider implications of science and technology upon the whole human race rather than in regard to development only. In this connection, *Tinbergen* noted that industrial and underdeveloped countries might in many instances have similar interests in developing new technologies, and mentioned as an example labour-intensive technologies, which were definitely needed in developing countries and that might also improve the existing income distribution in many developed countries. He also remarked that in spite of a general belief to the contrary, multinational corporations in many cases did have an interest in developing technologies that could also be applied in developing countries and that while the main emphasis in development programs must be on public activity, private interest can also contribute.

Fawcett, in connection with a remark from Gresford concerning the possibility of preventing infractions upon human rights through the application of modern science and technology, stated that it was quite unrealistic to believe that it would be possible to control the uses of technology through formal agreements and international conventions. In such agreements governments would always put in all types of legal reservations and qualifications in order to safeguard their own possible interests. As an example he mentioned that in one year alone 1200 surveillances had been legally authorized in spite of their being generally forbidden by international convention. An especially disturbing element in this connection was that people so obviously did not care about the problem of misuse of technology.

Blix suggested that one should try to focus the discussion on one thing at the time and proposed that one should proceed by attempting to determine the extent to which there is dissatisfaction with the current direction in research and the possibility for giving it a new direction by pointing out problems in areas in which there was a real need to concentrate research activities. Then one could discuss which means and stimulants to use. *Buzzati-Traverso* pointed out that the reports of ACAST (Advisory Committee on Application of Science and Technology to Development) gives listings of problems to which not enough attention has been given and that they also give suggestions for actions that should be taken. The literature is therefore available and identification of problem areas is not difficult. It is nevertheless true that action still has not been taken, and he saw the cause for this in the facts that (1) everybody first and foremost looks to his own interests, (2) most scientists have their own pet projects and do not want to be disturbed by other tasks and (3) the disorganized state of scientific activity at the international level prevents organized action being taken.

King saw one cause of the difficulty in the facts that problems of science and of aid are not discussed in overall science policy forums and that discussion of new programs for developing countries are usually restricted to the professional aid agencies without adequate participation from scientists. In addition, he noted, most countries resent allocation of funds to international science programs because those funds will in most cases be taken from those resources that are allocated to their internal problems. He mentioned that a few years ago OECD had tried to launch a campaign for a science of aid program for development in a broad multidisciplinary sense in contrast to the existing approach of applying science to solve single and fractionalized problems, but this had not been accepted by the participating governments. *Buzzati-Traverso* noted, in this connection, that one cannot expect governments with their particular organizations and interests to be able or willing to create a science for development. This can only be done by the scientists themselves. They mut be made aware of the problem and they must 'band together' to solve it.

Hedén found King's statement that one cannot expect development from governments discouraging and shared Buzzati-Traverso's hope that efforts from the scientists themselves might lead to the necessary changes. Noting Tinbergen's statement on the role of multinational corporations, he remarked that those corporations might indeed be more conducive to change than governments because the main concern of corporations is survival and their survival is to a large extent dependent upon the markets that can be developed in the present poor countries. In connection with remarks from Blix and Seaborg concerning the apparent success of WHO (World Health Organization) he pointed out that delegations to WHO are homogeneous, consisting of medical and health personnel, while in other international agencies delegations are heterogeneous. In those instances they do not have identical interests nor do they 'speak the same language'; and they do not act together or through the same channels in their own national apparatus. For this reason he believed that it would be much easier to get an international science policy if national science policies could be established first.

Dahl was rather sceptical about the possibility of establishing a general global research policy and pointed out that research and development are in fact different types of activity. When one moves from science into technology the real problems become the questions of financing, of management and of politics and those are different from the questions the scientist tries to find answers to. He felt there-

118

fore that it would be easier to reach agreement on what one should not do than to establish a policy for positive action. *Randers* elaborated further on the question of a science policy and asked what was really meant by it; was it a set of guidelines regulating government support to science? or a policy for the application of scientific results? or was it to be a policy on the use of science to aid developing countries? While sympathizing with the various causes and needs, he nevertheless felt questions of help to the developing countries was too wide a subject to be covered by the Symposium. If, on the other hand, science policy was understood to govern public support to science and the question of priorities among the various disciplines, that would be a manageable problem to debate, e.g. by asking if a time had now come when the social sciences should be given higher priority than before and expansion in the natural sciences be contained?

Hambro, who was the last speaker in this part of the discussion, found it surprising that some of the speakers apparently felt that there were no problems that were global in the sense that they would require globally applicable solutions. In his opinion, such problems as environment, population growth and ocean space were definitely global in scale and of a kind where solutions could only be found through international cooperation at a global scale. He was also surprised to find that some of the participants expressed doubt with regard to the value and importance of interdisciplinary cooperation. From his own experience he must emphasize the need for diplomats and international lawyers to have collaboration from scientists and technical experts. While diplomats may be experts in putting substantive rules into the proper legal framework, they are ignorant in substantive matters where scientists have the knowledge but lack the ability to formulate rules and regulations.

With *King*'s paper on the OECD approach to scientific and technological cooperation and the oral presentation by *Randers* of the activities of NATO in this field, the question of coordination of activities of diverse regional organizations, as well as the question of their proper spheres of activity, became subjects for discussion. *Gardner* claimed that such organizations of industrialized countries as OECD, ECE, the Council of Europe and NATO to a large extent duplicate each other's work when they are active, for instance, in environment affairs and scientific matters. He also claimed that the only justification for an environment program in an organization like NATO was a political one, as a means to legitimate the alliance. *Randers,* on the other hand, found it quite natural that when NATO countries did find that they shared a common interest in pursuing the environment problem, they should do so. The fact that environment was also a concern to countries outside NATO should not prevent member countries from acting within their own organization. He also pointed out that scientists from non-member countries were often invited to participate in NATO activities in the field of science. *King* acknowledged that in a formal sense cooperation between OECD and NATO was made difficult by the fact that non-NATO countries are also members of OECD. In practice, however, such formal difficulties could be overcome by personal contacts, and duplication could be avoided. Neither was there really any duplication of activities between OECD and the Council of Europe or ECE, where quite harmonious relations prevailed. Yet even if there were no duplication he nevertheless thought that if the resources now allocated to science and research through all these regional organizations were to be deployed under a joint and coordinated plan, the same funds might give a result possibly as much as three times better than under the present system.

In the context of the activities of these regional organizations the problem of developing countries also proved to be a major issue. *Kristensen* found that it was a major reason for concern that the scientific resources of the rich countries are so overwhelmingly spent upon their own internal problems and that, while in recent years there had been an increasing concern over global problems, the interest in and support for poor countries had nevertheless been stagnant or even decreasing. *Hambro,* while agreeing that it was right and necessary for developed countries to help the less fortunate nations, nevertheless felt that it was necessary to point out that the emphasis on the problem of the developing countries must not be taken to mean that development aid should be the one and exclusive interest to be served by scientific cooperation. It would be dangerous, he said, to allow oneself to be caught in a development syndrome. *King* fully agreed that scientific cooperation for the purpose of development must not be put in a unique position, but he also pointed out that too small a proportion of the total resources are currently used for development purposes. Thus, as a 'club of donor countries' OECD should devote more attention to the question of mobilizing a scientific effort in the development process.

As will be readily apparent even from this brief and incomplete summary of the substantive part of the discussion at the Symposium a very wide range of problems was covered. While there were individual differences in the opinions expressed on many of the issues, in most instances these proved to be differences in emphasis rather than of substantive opinion. Above all there was a uniform agreement that solution of many of the problems that were discussed would be decisive for the future of mankind and, furthermore, that it was essential that scientists and technologists play an active role toward making such solutions possible, at the international as well as at the national level.

While none of the questions could be debated in full detail the participants nevertheless felt that a number of conclusions could be drawn from the presentations that had been made and from the discussion of the various problems. The last part of the discussion, therefore, was concentrated on the question of what conclusions one should draw from Nobel Symposium 26:

In the Symposium it was recognized that the general trend moves toward a concept of global development in an ever more strongly integrated world where an increasing number of problems become world-wide. While in most instances such problems are not susceptible to uniform solutions, they must nevertheless be solved on a global scale. In this situation interdisciplinary collaboration of scientists and technologists must continue and be expanded on an international basis, and special emphasis should be given to the serious shortage of research on problems that are specific to the poorer part of the world.

Among the global problems that require coordinated research special note was taken of the following: population growth, food shortages, water supply, energy requirements, the organization of oceanic space, the protection of the human environment, the provision of housing, compatible urban growth, the fight against poverty and underdevelopment in all parts of the world, the betterment of health, all of which will contribute to improving the quality of life for all mankind.

It was deemed essential that all relevant information concerning these questions and the opportunities offered by scientific research and technological development be made available to statesmen and diplomats in such a way that it could help lay the foundations for constructive international as well as national policies. In this connection, it was emphasized that there is a need for greater parliamentary understanding — and control — of scientific research and technological development while at the same time the scientific community must be made better aware of the needs for and advantages of coordination of research in relation to problems that are global in scale.

In regard to the role of the specialized agencies of the UN in the field of science and technology, it was felt that a critical, external review and evaluation of the structure, management and activities of those agencies and of the many UN committees might prove helpful toward rationalizing their operations and mobilizing scientists and technologists in a coordinated effort to attack and solve vital problems.

There is also a need for the UN system as a whole, as well as for national governments, to have an overview assessment on a regular basis of such trends of development as constitute threats and opportunities in a long-range perspective (10—20 years). For this purpose a Commission of the Future might perform a useful and necessary function.

It was felt that the emerging UN University, if properly organized, could play an important role in providing a new forum for interdisciplinary, as well as international scientific cooperation. In this connection, it was pointed out that the scientific community itself must take a leading role in developing the new university and that the best results would be achieved through a flexible organization with a maximum of intellectual autonomy and a minimum of international bureaucracy.

Finally, it was felt that voluntary, non-governmental organizations and associations should play an active role toward improved interdisciplinary and international coordination in the field of science and technology, and increased research on the various vital problems mentioned above, including those which are specific to the developing countries. In this connection, new structures, such as those emerging in an International Foundation for Science (IFS) for the support of young scientists in less developed countries and the International Federation of Institutes for Advanced Study (IFIAS) were welcome as fresh evidence of the awareness among scientists of the problems facing man on an international and global scale and of their active search for ways and means to meet this challenge.

As mentioned in the Opening Address practically all invited accepted the invitation to participate in the Symposium. Unfortunately shortly before the Symposium started several of the persons invited informed the Institute that they were not able to come. These were: Carlos Chagas, Brazil, Jermen M. Guishiani, USSR, Wilfred Jenks, Great Britain, Manfred Lachs, Poland, Maurice Strong, Canada, Victor Urquidi, Mexico.

LIST OF PARTICIPANTS

Hans Blix,
Counsellor, Ministry of Foreign
  Affairs,
Stockholm, Sweden.

Norman E. Borlaug,
Director, International Maize and
  Wheat Improvement Center,
Mexico.

Adriano Buzzati-Traverso,
Professor,
Lungotevere Mellini, 34, 000193,
Rome.

Helmer Dahl,
Director of Research, Christian
  Michelsen Institute,
Bergen, Norway.

J. E. S. Fawcett,
23, Hanover House,
  St. John's Wood High Street,
London.

Richard Gardner,
Professor, School of Geography,
Oxford University, Oxford.

Guy B. Gresford,
Director for Science and Technology,
  United Nations,
Present address: Department of
  Foreign Affairs, Canberra A.C.T.
  Australia.

Edvard Hambro,
Ambassador, Délégation de Norvège,
Geneva.

Carl-Göran Hedén,
Professor, Caroline Institute,
Stockholm.

Alexander King,
Director for Scientific Research,
  OECD,
Paris.

Thorkil Kristensen,
Professor, Institute for Development
  Research,
Copenhagen.

Koichi Mera,
The International Development Center of Japan,
Tokyo.

Dr. Sam Nilsson,
Secretary General, IFIAS,
Stockholm.

Gunnar Randers,
Assistant Secretary-General, Division
  of Scientific Affairs, NATO,
Brussels.

Abdus Salam,
Professor, International Center for
  Theoretical Physics,
Trieste.

John Sanness,
Professor, Norwegian Institute of
  International Affairs,
Oslo.

August Schou,
Director, Norwegian Nobel Institute,
Oslo.

Glenn Seaborg,
Professor, University of California,
Berkeley.

Finn Sollie,
Director, The Fridtjof Nansen
  Foundation Polhøgda,
Oslo.

Nils K. Ståhle,
Envoyé, President of IFIAS,
Stockholm.

Jan Tinbergen,
Professor, Erasmus University of
  Rotterdam,
Rotterdam.

Organizing Committee:
  August Schou,
  John Sanness,
  Finn Sollie.

NOBEL FOUNDATION SYMPOSIUM COMMITTEE

Ramel, Stig, Chairman, Executive Director of the Nobel Foundation.

Hulthén, Lamek, Professor, Member of the Nobel Committee for Physics.

Fredga, Arne, Professor emer., Chairman of the Nobel Committee for Chemistry.

Gustafsson, Bengt, Professor, Secretary of the Nobel Committee for Medicine.

Gyllensten, Lars, Professor, Member of the Nobel Committee of the Swedish Academy (literature).

Schou, August, Director of the Norwegian Nobel Institute (peace).

Ohlin, Bertil, Professor emer., Chairman of the Committee for the Prize in Economic Science in Memory of Alfred Nobel.